JASON KARL'S GREAT GHOST HUNT

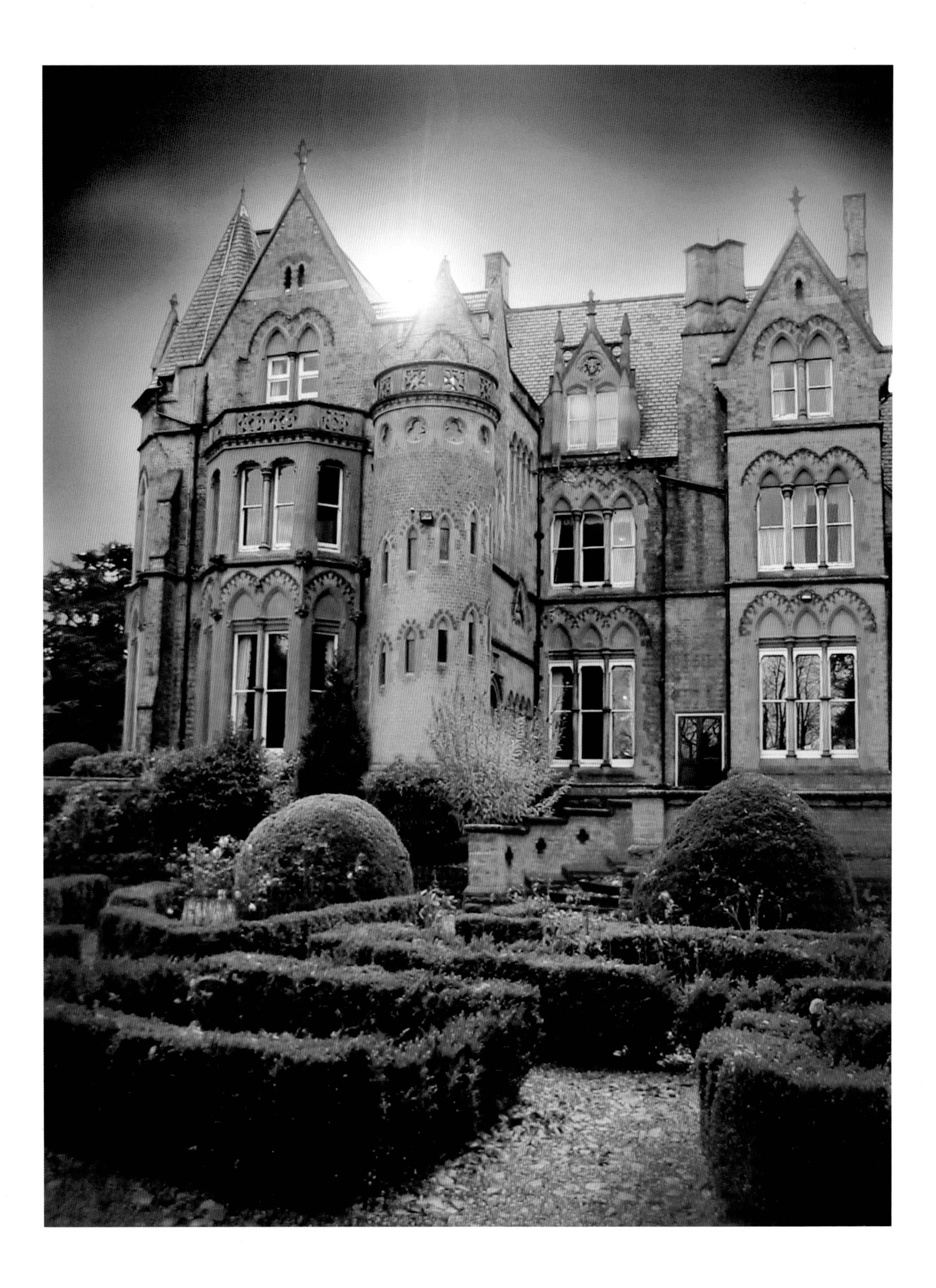

JASON KARL'S GREAT GHOST HUNT

This edition published in 2005 by New Holland Publishers (UK) Ltd
London • Cape Town • Sydney • Auckland

www.newhollandpublishers.com

Garfield House, 86–88 Edgware Road, London W2 2EA,
United Kingdom

80 McKenzie Street, Cape Town 8001, South Africa

14 Aquatic Drive, Frenchs Forest, NSW 2086, Australia

218 Lake Road, Northcote, Auckland, New Zealand

10 9 8 7 6 5 4 3 2

ISBN 1 84537 430 4 (paperback)
ISBN 1 84330 735 9 (hardback)

Publishing Manager: Jo Hemmings
Senior Editor: Kate Michell
Copy Editor: Deborah Taylor
Assistant Editor: Rose Hudson
Indexer: Dorothy Frame
Cover Design and Design: Alan Marshall
Production: Joan Woodroffe

Reproduction by Pica Digital Pte Ltd, Singapore
Printed and bound by Star Standard (Singapore) Pte Ltd

Photographs appearing on the cover and prelim pages are as follows:
Front cover: Chillingham Castle, Northumberland; back cover: Muncaster Castle, Cumbria (courtesy of Muncaster Castle); page 2: Bestwood Lodge Hotel, Nottinghamshire; opposite: Athelhampton Hall, Dorset; contents: Chillingham Castle, Northumberland; page 11: Leap Castle, County Offaly, Ireland

DEDICATION

This book is dedicated to everyone who has been involved with The Ghost Research Foundation International since its genesis in 1992, and especially to my partner Simon Castle for tirelessly putting up with me and my ghosts!

Contents

Foreword

Parapsychology is fortunate in having Jason Karl; a young, enthusiastic, open-minded and responsible investigator and organizer, whose work should ensure that the unbiased and scientific exploration of haunted houses will continue for the foreseeable future. At the same time, I am sure that in this book the author fervently wishes his readers a few uncomfortable moments and he does not disappoint. Whether you are an armchair investigator or a field-worker in this fascinating realm, *Jason Karl's Great Ghost Hunt* is essential and enthralling reading.

Definitions

Definitions can be dangerous, but if a ghostly apparition is a supernatural appearance of a person who is deceased or elsewhere (and there is evidence of ghosts of living persons), and if the evidence for such appearances is good, then examination of this area of human experience must be important. There can be no doubt that, even in this prosaic age, men and women who are sound in mind and body do sometimes see ghosts in circumstances that rule out illusion and deception. And the evidence is certainly good: from every corner of the world, in every society and community and in every kind of human experience since the beginning of civilization, there is overwhelming proof that what we call ghosts exist. Now, all we have to do is prove their existence scientifically, and books such as *Jason Karl's Great Ghost Hunt* help towards this end.

The Evidence for Ghosts is an in-depth exploration of the types of ghosts and ghostly activity that might be encountered. This is an important chapter, as ghost investigation is inevitably coloured by the outlook, experience and objectivity of the investigator concerned and today, when there are more people who believe in the reality of paranormal activity than who accept the existence of an omnipotent god, Jason Karl is a welcome guide to these absorbing regions.

'Most haunted'?

I am fortunate in having personal memories of most of the places included in Britain's Most Haunted Places. For me, many passages brought back some of those rare moments in life when you are aware of a glimpse, an impression, a comprehension, a knowledge of something beyond normal everyday life. True ghostly experiences result in the arresting conviction that this familiar workaday world of ours may have strange, and possibly terrifying, holes in it. All may not be exactly as it seems.

The question of authenticity is overwhelmingly important. If what we see is hallucination or the result of imagination we know what to do, but if it is not, what then?

The interesting Hoel Fanog haunting came to my attention years ago. Absorbing as it appears to be, I have to say I have always had some reservations. I have always tried to avoid saying any house is 'the most haunted'; after all such a statement means little without qualification and definition: haunted because of the intensity and ferocity of the disturbances; because of the variety of phenomena; because of the length of time over which the disturbances occurred; because of the number of people who experienced the happenings; because of the effect of the disturbances; because of the scientific investigation of what has been going on? And tomorrow a new haunting may come along to eclipse anything previously reported.

I have talked to Eddie Burks, the renowned 'releaser of trapped souls' who works in collaboration with the London College of Psychic Studies, about this case at some length. He certainly seems to have been instrumental in lifting the oppressive atmosphere and getting life back to normal there.

So, haunted a house may be but 'the most haunted' is difficult to substantiate and, personally, I think it is unwise to define any property as such. After all, what may be regarded as haunted by one person may be considered by another to be affected by the presence of a certain person or persons, by physical and geophysical features or by opportunism. The fact remains that the Heol Fanog case in the beautiful Brecon Beacons could still repay close examination.

I had the pleasure of knowing Roy Harley Lewis who initially explored the mysteries of Littledean Hall in the mysterious and attractive Forest of Dean, and from him and the one-time owner and occupier Donald Macer-Wright I heard first hand the many tales of ghosts and ghostly activity that at one time cried out for serious and scientific investigation. The Ghost Club Society tried but sadly no such examination of the property and its inhabitants, both human and supernatural, was ever conducted, so we are left with weird and wonderful reported happenings that linger in the memory, tinged with regret for an opportunity missed.

I discussed at considerable length the psychic activity reported at Ettington Park, a Victorian Gothic pile in Warwickshire, with a number of relevant people, including Jenny Bright and her husband scientist Dr David Cross who together carried out a psychic survey of the property. Jenny was commissioned to do this work, which resulted in the publication of *The Hidden Heritage of Ettingdon Park*, following her success as a professional psychic and medium. At Ettington Park Jenny confirmed some of the long-accepted ghost stories, clarified others and established some new ones. She believes the stories of a ghostly Grey Lady, long-known to staff and guests at the present hotel, actually represents two separate hauntings that over time have become entwined into a single story: all intriguing stuff! I see my files on Ettington Park go back to 1956 – it's time I visited again!

Pengersick Castle in Cornwall is certainly haunted. I have been friends with the owner Angela Evans for many years now and the Ghost Club Society has conducted a number of remarkable and singularly successful all-night studies at Pengersick. At one such study in 1997, seven members of the ten-member team saw ghostly figures.

Pluckley in Kent was long dubbed by the press as 'England's most haunted village'; now that accolade seems to have descended on Prestbury in the Cotswolds, and deservedly so. With a myriad of reported ghostly forms, from the English Civil War (1842–9) and earlier, altogether there are at least 20 tales of apparent hauntings in the village, more than sufficient, it seems to me, to warrant serious consideration. The review in this book of Prestbury's ghosts is probably the best and most exhaustive ever compiled.

I think I may have been the first to bring wide attention to the hauntings associated with The Wellington Hotel at Boscastle, where my wife and I spent holidays twice a year for many years. More than 20 years ago I personally explored the ghostly happenings reported from this delightful 16th-century coaching inn and I have no doubts that disturbing occurrences have taken place there.

Favourite Haunts

Jason Karl awards Berry Pomeroy Castle with the title of 'the second most haunted castle in Britain' and perhaps he is right. Certainly, I have no argument with his conclusions that for years this place has been the scene of countless encounters with something not of this world and that it is a place that once visited can never be forgotten.

The other 'favourite haunts' of the author of this excellent book include an ancient cottage in Devon; grand and quietly beautiful Athelhampton Hall in Dorset, where I have fond memories of being the guest of Robert Cooke MP; an ancient inn in Gloucestershire; an isolated former farmhouse in Essex and haunted places in Wales, Scotland and Ireland for good measure.

Helpful Hints for Haunted Houses

A useful guide follows and tells you how to decide whether you actually live in a haunted house; there is a chapter on time slips and details of more than 20 hotels where you might share a room with a ghost! The book ends with a Glossary, a valuable Bibliography and several useful Witness Report and Interview Forms. In *Jason Karl's Great Ghost Hunt* the author tells us what he has done, suggests what we might do and points out the pitfalls; he bids us welcome to his world but with the appropriate warnings.

It may be that, in the majority of haunted houses, what ghosts achieve when they appear, as Henry James once said, is scarcely consistent with their taking the trouble – and an immense trouble they find it, we gather, to appear at all. However, surely the point is that they do appear. If we are to accept human testimony, which is accepted in a court of law, then to find out as much as we can on this important matter is surely the duty of us all.

All in all, Jason Karl is to be congratulated on a hauntingly good read – especially for the hours after midnight!

Peter Underwood
Life President of the Ghost Club Society

Introduction

This book is about ghosts – the ghosts of Great Britain to be precise – and my 12-year hunt to find them: my Great Ghost Hunt.

My first encounter with a ghost was when I was 13, it was an experience that has never left me and was both fascinating and terrifying. It was this incident that led me to seek out books on the subject and I soon discovered the works of Peter Underwood – the undisputed King of Ghost Hunters. It was Peter's books that were both my inspiration and my reference when I first began to visit and investigate haunted houses. During my years of research I have lived in a haunted stately home, been 'attacked' by a phantom monk, investigated a haunted sex club, and spent literally thousands of hours poised in darkened chambers waiting eagerly for a visitation from beyond.

Do I believe in ghosts? The answer is, of course, yes. But exactly what ghosts are is a different question. I believe that people have experiences that cannot be explained within the parameters of current science, but whether those experiences are always caused by something in the external environment or are occasionally something from within us is an enigma that has not yet been resolved. The weight of evidence for ghosts is enormous and belief in the supernatural can be traced back thousands of years. Ghosts are a cross-cultural phenomenon and seem to ignore all boundaries of class, gender and even the laws of time itself.

This book is not an account of my case studies, it is a general work of reference in which you will find accounts of some of my favourite haunted places, information about how you can become a ghost hunter yourself and the first ever published ghost classification system, in which I have attempted to categorize all types of ghostly phenomena in a usable and easy-to-follow format.

For those brave enough to venture out into the haunted world, I have included a section on Britain's most haunted places and another on ghost-ridden hotels. If you do plan to visit any of these places, please remember to respect others' privacy and to ensure that you do not trespass onto private property. I have found that owners of haunted locations are usually more than happy to entertain your pursuit if you approach them in a direct and polite manner. There is also a section on timeslips – the most fascinating of all ghostly encounters.

This book is the result of my research so far, and everything in it is presented as I have found it. Everything here is my opinion, formed as a result of my research and that of the Ghost Research Foundation International (GRFI), which I co-founded in Oxford in 1992, and of which I am now a Life Patron.

Ghosts are a good reason to visit any historical site in Britain, but they are by no means the only reason to seek out the country's haunted heritage. Britain is an ancient land dotted with crumbling manor houses, monastic abbeys and moated castles, which stretch from the rocky coast of Cornwall to the Highlands and Islands of Scotland, each a unique gem harbouring a fascinating history and, of course, many great ghost stories.

Happy Ghost Hunting!

Jason Dexter Karl
www.jasondexterkarl.com

The Evidence for Ghosts

GHOST MANIFESTATION

Following my studies of ghosts and hauntings, I believe that ghosts manifest in four stages and that they require energy to progress through these stages. Energy seems to be obtained by a ghost from one or more of the following sources:

Electricity Supply

A ghost's need for electricity explains why some haunted locations have inexplicably high or fluctuating electricity bills. One such case occurred at Heol Fanog, a haunted farmhouse in the Brecon Beacons, where the Rich family experienced a wealth of phenomena, including bills of up to £750 per quarter.

Witnesses often report electrical malfunctions in haunted houses, such as appliances switching themselves on or off and lights dimming and flickering of their own accord. Such occurrences are due to the ghost or ghosts feeding off the electricity supply.

Above: *A full apparition appeared in this photograph behind the seated girl, despite not being witnessed at the time.*

Battery Power

In many hauntings, witnesses report that battery-powered devices, such as tape recorders, TV cameras, video equipment and lights, fail to work and that, on inspection, even new and recently charged batteries are found to be dead. Battery energy can be harnessed by ghosts and used to aid manifestation, yet how they drain the power from batteries remains unknown.

Human Energy Field

The human brain produces a form of energy, and it is thought that this can be harnessed by a ghost to help it progress through the four stages of manifestation. Witnesses of supernatural phenomena often report feeling tired or drained after the experience, and this is probably because the entity is taking energy from the witness.

In some circumstances, a conducive atmosphere for manifestation can be created by having lots of people, particularly young people, present. The presence of young people is more conducive possibly because they have a stronger bio-electric energy field than older people; this may also explain why children under the age of 10 are more likely to see ghosts than people of other ages.

Evidence to support this theory includes a roll of photographic film that was taken at a party in 1997. The photographs show a Stage 1 and a Stage 2 ghost following a child around various rooms. The entity is only visible on the photographs in which the child appears as it was latching onto the strongest energy field at the party.

Above: *Ley lines criss-cross the planet and are thought to conduct psychic paranormal energies.*

Bearing this in mind, it is beneficial when attempting a séance or trying to communicate with a presence for a strong energy source to be available for the ghost to use. Investigators can achieve this by getting everyone present to form a circle by linking hands or touching fingers and then asking them to concentrate on the energy flowing through their bodies from left to right. In this human circle, the energy comes from a collective energy source, which lessens the chance of any one person feeling exhausted at the end.

Research has also suggested that the presence of a psychic or medium can be beneficial as they seem to have a higher energy field, which is why they sometimes experience ghosts at stages of manifestation that the average person cannot sense. Sufferers of epilepsy also seem particularly conducive to paranormal occurrences. During my research, I have explored possible reasons for this and it has been suggested that the brain patterns of an epileptic give off more energy than the brain patterns of a non-epileptic and ghosts are attracted to this potent energy source. This may also be part of the reason why many people with psychiatric problems or who experience high levels of stress seem to induce poltergeist phenomena.

Ley Lines

Ghost researchers know that locations directly on or near ley lines are prone to paranormal events, especially in places where two or more ley lines cross. These ley-line convergences are called window areas. Magnetic polarities on ley lines seem to be unstable and an investigator can observe this by placing a compass on the ley line or window area. The unusual effect of ley lines on magnetic energy may explain why ghosts seem to dwell at these areas.

Theories as to exactly what ley lines are vary, but one belief is that they are magnetic fault-lines connecting ancient or sacred sites such as religious buildings, burial grounds and wells. Why these sites were built in straight lines is unknown, but the popular theory is that our ancestors were more psychically aware of the *genius loci* – the feeling of a place. The natural energy led our ancestors to believe that these were good places to locate important buildings or religious sites.

Many buildings and locations standing on ley-line intersections have incredibly strong energy fields. If the energy is negative it can cause depression and other adverse degenerative medical conditions. Negative ley-line locations also seem to attract evil influences.

On the other hand, positive ley-line locations can perform apparently miraculous events, such as the healing of the sick. They can also benefit those who dwell on, or near them and in many cases simply being at these locations can induce a feeling of euphoria.

Ley lines can be a powerful source of energy for entities attempting to progress through the four stages of manifestation, but ley-line energy flow seems to fluctuate according to many outside influences, including meteorological conditions and natural electrical atmospheres.

Black Streams

We know that energy is either positive or negative and that positive energy attracts positive energy and negative energy attracts negative energy. In most cases, the energy that flows along ley lines seems to be positive. However, if a ley line hits a negative location, that is one that is inhabited by a negative, evil or malevolent conscious entity or a location that has witnessed high levels of torment and tragedy, it is possible for the energy field of that location to become negative.

Once a site has become negative it seems to feed only on negative energies and thus attracts negative spirits. Ley lines on negative sites become black streams, and the *genius loci* often becomes foreboding, unpleasant, gloomy and, in extreme cases, frightening. The effects in this situation are not caused by a ghost but by the presence of negative energy. However, if a negative entity is also present, this can worsen the effect. Some locations on black streams suffer high levels of frightening or unpleasant psychic phenomena, but it is important to remember that most ghost entities do not cause direct harm to the living, and the most common way for ghosts to harm a person is by creating intense fear.

Meteorological Conditions

During my research, I have found that higher amounts of supernatural activity occur during the autumn and winter. Investigations have concluded that this is because climatic weather conditions affect energy levels in the atmosphere, which in turn affects the energy sources available to ghosts.

Storms are caused by natural electrical energies, which is another source of power available to the manifesting entity. Ghost phenomena are often experienced during stormy weather, high winds, heavy rain or a mixture of these. Unusual or extreme weather conditions create changes in the general atmosphere, which appear to be extremely conducive to ghost manifestations. Having said that, this is just one available energy source, and ghosts are experienced in all types of weather and climates.

Bearing these six energy sources in mind, the best place to witness a Stage 4 materialization would be in a haunted house sited on a ley line with a group of happy young people during a storm! This is, of course, an unlikely scenario (although I have found myself in this very situation one several occasions!). Basically, the more energy sources available, the better your chances of seeing a ghost are.

Above: *Ghosts seem to manifest in four separate stages, Stages 1 to 3 seen here from left to right. Stage 1: Energy Genesis; Stage 2: Energy Vortex; Stage 3: Ectoplasm Formation.*

THE FOUR STAGES OF GHOST MANIFESTATION

STAGE 1: Energy Genesis or Orb

These are often found on photographs taken at haunted locations and can be identified from several features.

Energy genesis takes on the appearance of a mass that appears translucent at the edges but more solid at the centre. Energy masses vary in colour, and there are white, red, pink, orange, grey, blue and black examples of Stage 1 manifestations. Some psychics have expressed the belief that energy masses of black appearance are negative entities or malevolent ghosts. When Stage 1 manifestations occur, witnesses often see pinpoints of light in varying colours darting around the air. The most common colours reported are white and azure blue. Flashes of light, very much like those caused by a camera flash-bulb, are also often reported.

Energy masses vary in size and will often constantly alter their shape and substance. Evidence of this has been found on sets of photographs showing the mass moving and altering on consecutive prints. Energy masses levitate in ether and can move at any speed.

I have not found any evidence to suggest that a Stage 1 ghost can communicate with the living on any level. Stage 1 ghosts do not have enough energy to produce any phenomena other than pinpoint lights and orbs. When a Stage 1 phenomenon appears on photographic film it is often called 'the Casper effect', because of its similarity to the fictional ghost character of the same name. Temperature and magnetic variations do not seem to occur very often in the presence of an energy mass, and they cannot usually by seen with the naked eye.

TRANSITION Ghosts in transition from Stage 1 to 2 appear on photographs as streaks of colour that look as if they are moving quickly in one direction. These streaks usually appear as white, dark grey, black, green, blue or red on photographs. They sometimes show features of Stage 1 or 2 manifestations.

STAGE 2: Energy Vortex

As with Stage 1, an energy vortex often appears on photographs taken at haunted sites, but its appearance is radically different. It manifests as a cylindrical tube or coil, which normally hovers and moves vertically. Very few examples of an energy vortex show it moving horizontally. There appears to be a dense fluid within the tubular coil that mingles incessantly with itself. Stage 2 manifestations are nearly always white or azure blue, but occasionally they have been seen in pink or dark grey. As with Stage 1 manifestations, Stage 2 appearances can rarely be seen by the naked

Above: *A fully manifested Stage 4 apparition can be seen standing by the door at the back of this early 20th-century photograph taken in a pottery.*

eye; normally they only appear on photographs.

A Stage 2 manifestation was experienced by the Keeper of the Crown Jewels in the Tower of London on a Saturday in 1817. Stage 2 entities are detectable by investigators because they cause magnetic changes and temperature variations when they are present. Stage 2 manifestations can also show signs of intelligence and have been known to interact with ghost investigators.

At Chingle Hall in Lancashire, a ghost hunter detected a presence from a cold spot and took a photograph of the area. He then asked the ghost to follow him inside the building and then took another photograph of the interior. Both photographs show the Stage 2 paranormal energy coil, the second showing slightly stronger than the first. This evidence shows that the entity could hear and understand him, and that it was able to follow his request.

TRANSITION Stage 2 to Stage 3 transitions often reveal the addition of one or more thin strands or rods, like thick pieces of string, within the fluid area of the coil. This is the beginning of the third stage of manifestation.

STAGE 3: Ectoplasm Formation

If sufficient energy is available to the entity, it progresses to take on a sub-physical form. This ethereal presence can be caught on photographs and videotape and has an azure or grey swirling smoke-like appearance. It often resembles the shape of a figure or face, but more often it creates the outline or silhouette of an apparition. At this stage, the ghost can make physical contact with the living through tactual phenomena, and can cause spectral scents and psychic breezes. The spectral scents are likely to be relevant to the identity of the ghost.

Temperature and magnetic variations are nearly always recorded in the presence of Stage 3 manifestations. Psychics can sense the presence of a ghost at any stage of manifestation, but it can be sensed particularly strongly at Stage 3. Flashlights or camera flashes often highlight Stage 3 entities so that they become visible to the human eye. Stage 3 manifestations move like smoke although they are erratic, ranging from slow speeds to sudden and spasmodic movement.

At this stage of manifestation, the entity shows signs of intelligent interaction, as at Stage 2, and can also induce aural phenomena such as raps, knockings, screams and footfall. Stage 3 manifestations can be seen without the aid of photography, although they are nearly always seen in the presence of camera flashlight.

TRANSITION Between Stages 3 and 4, a ghost makes the most noticeable changes in its form.

STAGE 4: Manifestation/ Materialization

This is the final stage of a ghost's progress to manifestation. If enough energy has been available to the entity it will be able to manifest fully. However, completely manifested ghosts are still not always visible to the human eye.

At this stage, the ghost is an apparition – something that appears fully manifest on photographs even though it may not have been seen when the picture was taken. For an apparition to materialize, it requires an enormous amount of energy. When it materializes, the ghost's structure somehow changes and becomes physically real. In this way, the living can interact physically with it.

If an apparition becomes visible to the human eye, whether it is fully materialized or not, it can appear as anything from a whispy, transparent entity to a form that is translucent or solid. Similarly, it could take the form of a human figure, an animal or something indefinable.

Above: *The ghost of Lady Hoby is said to step out from her portrait in negative form. The portrait hangs at Bisham Abbey in Berkshire.*

Descriptions of full manifestations vary from case to case and cover a wide range of visual forms. More unusual hauntings appear in the shape of dismembered human limbs.

Other notable apparitions appear as shapeless masses and come in numerous colours. These are often described by witnesses as similar in movement and appearance to mercury. Human apparitions sometimes appear in black and white or negative form – a term coined because of its similarity to a negative photograph. The ghost of Lady Hoby at Bisham Abbey in Berkshire is one example of a negative ghost.

Another regular feature reported by witnesses is of ghosts appearing without eyes, but rather with two black sockets staring alarmingly back at the observer. This often induces even greater fear in what is already a frightening experience.

At Stage 4, a ghost is at its most powerful and can perform all the phenomena reported in Stages 1, 2 and 3 but with greater strength. The sounds it makes are likely to be louder and the scents it produces stronger. They can also interact physically with the living, but with greater force than at Stage 3. Stage 4 materializations can appear strongly on photographs and videotape. At Lancashire's Chingle Hall a phantom monk was caught on video floating down the staircase, even though he was not spotted at the time.

Security cameras have also been known to catch ghosts out, as at the Butterflies Nightclub in Oldham, Lancashire, where a ghost can clearly be seen moving along a corridor and through a locked door at the end. This particular videotape has been examined by experts, who have been unable to explain it in rational terms. The tape was recorded at 04:32 on October 27 1991, only four days before Hallowe'en, the day when the souls of the departed are believed to revisit their homes.

In January 1999, a ghost caught on video at Belgrave Hall in Leicestershire attracted a lot of media attention. It apparently shows a Stage 4 manifestation

which dissipates into a fog or mist before completely disappearing. Another fully manifested apparition was caught on tape in a supermarket in Penzance in autumn 2003; the tape shows a ghostly arm violently pushing cans of drink off a shelf.

Jamiroquai's lead singer, superstar **Jay Kay**, shares his Buckinghamshire mansion with a ghost of a lady dressed in green. Luga – his German shepherd dog – refuses to settle in a panelled room just next door to Jay Kay's bedroom. It is believed the ghost haunts this room and that she has visited Jay Kay during the night, holding him down so that he is temporarily unable to move.

Above: *At Chingle Hall in Lancashire a fully formed phantom monk was caught on video floating down the staircase.*

DISSIPATION/DEMATERIALIZATION

This can occur at any point during a manifestation for a number of reasons, including insufficient energy or the loss of a trigger individual's presence. One particularly effective way of dissipating any manifesting phenomena is to increase the amount of light in the area. No one knows why this has such a dramatic effect on ghosts, but it seems that some types of ghost are not conducive to light.

It is vital that all ghost hunters remember that psychics, mediums and some sensitive individuals can sense the presence of a ghost at any stage of manifestation. Although cameras and equipment are useful in recording phenomena, the information gleaned from these spiritually attuned people is important and should never be dismissed without first recording and later attempting to verify their statements.

GHOSTS AND THEIR EFFECT ON ANIMALS

Some animals are highly psychic and can sense ghosts. Animals can prove invaluable when ghosts are being investigated, as their reactions can help identify whether or not a haunting is taking place. American research into this area has shown that while cats and dogs are particularly sensitive to the presence of ghosts, some species of snake can also detect psychic atmospheres.

CATS AND GHOSTS

I have witnessed unusual behaviour by cats in many haunted places, including my own home. However, it seems that cats are like humans in that some are psychically perceptive and some are not.

Reactions include a cat seeming to be watching something move around an apparently empty room and sudden unjustified exits of otherwise favoured habitats as if something unpleasant has entered the space.

While living at a stately home in the north of England, I had a cat who was attuned to many of the ghosts said to haunt the building – he accompanied me through many nights of paranormal observance, often refusing to enter rooms.

DOGS AND GHOSTS

Dogs are even more sensitive to ghosts than cats, and it seems that all dogs are psychically perceptive. As with cats, dogs will watch invisible entities move around a room, refuse to enter certain rooms or areas and will bark, growl and snarl at thin air as if being challenged by something unseen.

Dematerialization Dissipation types

Ghosts dematerialize and dissipate in one of four ways:

Sudden Vanish The ghost is there one minute and gone the next!
Gradual Fade The ghost gradually fades into nothing, either quickly or slowly.
Out of View The ghost moves out of the percipient's view and, when followed, disappears.
Staggered Disappearance The ghost disappears in stages. In October 1952, the Rector of Langenhoe sighted a ghost that disappeared in this way. The ghost was of a woman in a cream dress. While the woman disappeared, the dress seemed to linger on before it also dematerialized.

Right: *Animals, particularly cats, are often sensitive to the presence of ghosts. My cat, Merlin, regularly accompanies me on ghost hunts.*

Haunters

WHAT EXACTLY IS A GHOST?

What exactly is a ghost? Is it a cold, inexplicable draught, a shadowy figure glimpsed on the stairs or a fork flying off the table into thin air? Or is it that peculiar scent that comes and goes without explanation? In fact it is all of these things – and more. The word 'ghost' is used to describe almost anything which we cannot explain.

The seven ghost categories

APPEARANCE, AWARENESS AND PERSONALITY CHARACTERISTICS OF GHOSTS	**Once-Sentient Ghosts**	**Inanimate Ghosts**	**Poltergeists**
	Ghosts of humans or animals that once lived	Ghosts of objects that have never been sentient	Location- and person-based poltergeists
INTERMITTENT	✓	✓	✓
CYCLIC	✓	✓	✓
ANNIVERSARY	✓	✓	✓
REACTIVE	✓	✓	✓
ONE-OFF	✓	✓	✓
CIRCULATIVE*	✓		
WANDERING*	✓		
CONSCIOUS**	✓		✓
OBLIVIOUS**	✓		✓
BENIGN***	✓	✓	✓
MALEVOLENT***	✓	✓	✓

* Ghosts *can be* CIRCULATIVE or WANDERING but are not necessarily so
** Ghosts *can be* CONSCIOUS or OBLIVIOUS
*** Ghosts *that are also* CONSCIOUS *can be* BENIGN or MALEVOLENT

We use the term 'ghost' for an entity with a personality that is usually invisible to the human eye and that appears to behave against all rules of logic and current scientific understanding.

As with humans, ghosts are unique and come in all shapes and sizes. Despite this, over the past 12 years I have tried to categorize ghosts into definitive groups and sub-groups along with phenomena profiles and awareness characteristics, and the result of this work is contained in the following pages. The groups are intended to be as exhaustive as possible and attempt to encompass all known ghost phenomena types. However, this grouping system is being continually edited and updated and, therefore, should not be relied upon to categorize all ghosts at any one time.

Over my years as a ghost researcher I have identified seven categories of ghost. While these groups have specific ghost types attributed to them, some ghosts could comfortably fit into several categories. In this instance, I have classified each ghost into the category that best suits their general activity. Any ghosts that do not fit into a standard category have been classified under the 'Miscellaneous Ghost Phenomena' category.

The seven categories are as follows:

	Doppelgängers	Timeslips	Elemental Ghosts	Miscellaneous Ghost Phenomena
	Human, animal and inanimate doppelgängers	All timeslip ghosts	Intelligent entities that have never been sentient	All other ghost phenomena
	✓	✓	✓	✓
	✓	✓	✓	✓
	✓	✓	✓	✓
	✓	✓	✓	✓
	✓	✓	✓	✓
				✓
				✓
	✓	✓	✓	✓
	✓	✓	✓	✓
			✓	✓
			✓	✓

GHOST CHARACTERISTICS EXPLAINED

Above: *The ghost of novelist Charles Dickens (1812–70) is a circulative ghost – he haunts several locations, including Doughty Street in London and the burial grounds at Rochester Castle in Kent.*

APPEARANCE CHARACTERISTICS

Intermittent Ghosts

Ghosts described as **intermittent** behave in no apparent pattern or routine. For example, the phenomena caused by an intermittent ghost entity may be experienced three times in one day and then not occur again for six months. This irregular behaviour is described as intermittent.

Cyclic Ghosts

Ghosts described as **cyclic** cause phenomena to occur at specific or regular times. For example, the phenomena caused by a cyclic ghost entity may always be experienced at the same time of day, or always on the same day of the week or month.

Anniversary Ghosts

Ghosts described as **anniversary** cause phenomena to occur on a day that was important during their sentient existence. For example, the ghost of Sir John Gate, which haunts Beeleigh Abbey in Maldon, Essex, is an anniversary ghost because he always appears on 11 August, presumably because this is close to the date (22 August) that Sir John was executed on Tower Hill, London in 1553. Anniversary ghosts, unlike cyclic ghosts, normally manifest themselves on a particular date, rather than a specific time of day or day in the week or month.

Reactive Ghosts

Ghosts described as **reactive** cause phenomena to occur as a reaction to an event or to actions taken by living people. For example, at Higher Farm in Chilton Cantelo, Somerset, the ghost lies dormant unless its skull is removed from the building. On removal of the skull a plethora of disturbing phenomena occur until the skull is returned to the house. This type of ghost entity is reactive because it does nothing unless incited to do so. Some types of reactive ghosts appear at times of crisis or emotional need for the witness.

One-off Ghosts

Ghosts described as being **one-off** cause phenomena to occur on just one occasion without any apparent reason for the timing of the phenomena.

Circulative Ghosts

Ghosts described as **circulative** haunt several different locations. Anne Boleyn's (1507–36) ghost is the best example of a circulative ghost. She haunts eight locations, including the Tower of London and Rochford Hall in Essex. Many circulative ghosts are also cyclic but this is not always the case. How or why some ghosts haunt many different places is unknown. Possibly they use ley lines to travel between locations or attach themselves to people who then carry them to a new location by paranormal induction. People who had powerful experiences in a number of places during their lifetime may haunt them later. The ghosts of novelist Charles Dickens (1812–70) and the explorer Sir Francis Drake (*c.* 1540–96) are other examples of circulative ghosts.

Wandering Ghosts

Ghosts described as **wandering** have been sighted at different locations but do not have a circulative pattern of haunting. They may have made one or two appearances at the same location or they may have appeared only at different locations and never returned to a site they have previously visited. They may use the same methods of moving around as circulative ghosts.

AWARENESS CHARACTERISTICS

Above: *Higher Farm at Chilton Cantelo in Somerset is home to the reactive ghost of one Theophilus Broome, whose skull still resides in the building. Theophilus creates ghostly phenomena only when his skull is removed from the farmhouse.*

Conscious Ghosts

Ghosts described as **conscious** seem to interact with the living. These ghosts have some sort of intelligence and are as aware of us as we are of them. Often they will be able to communicate in different ways, such as through a medium, a ouija board or by rapping on hard surfaces. They may also interact physically with the living, for example by stroking someone's hair.

Oblivious Ghosts

Ghosts described as **oblivious** seem to be unaware of the living world and exist in their own dimension without apparent intelligence or interaction with the living. Many researchers compare this type of ghost with a recording that is replayed under the right conditions. This may be the case, but it is equally likely that these ghosts are simply unaware of us or that they simply choose to ignore us.

PERSONALITY CHARACTERISTICS

Benign Ghosts

Most ghosts fall into the **benign** category. They do not seem to bring harm to the witness, rather, in many cases, they often actually benefit the witness in some way.

Malevolent Ghosts

In the living world there are good and bad people and it is much the same with ghosts. The personality of a person survives death and becomes part of the ghost. So, if a person has been grumpy or vengeful in life it is likely that they will retain that personality in the afterlife. **Malevolent** ghosts try to affect people's lives in negative ways. There are no recorded incidents of ghosts killing anyone, but there are records of them attempting to strangle, kick, scratch and throw people. These acts, though unpleasant, do not normally cause any real harm to the witness. In fact, it is much more likely that a malevolent ghost will harm its victim mentally rather than physically. Truly evil ghosts are just as rare as truly evil people, and therefore are not a great cause for concern.

Below: *Ouija boards are one way of reaching out to the spirit world, and through them contact has been made with many conscious ghosts.*

PHENOMENA PROFILES

Animal Phenomena

Irrational animal behaviour caused by the presence of ghosts. I once witnessed this at The Ancient Ram Inn in Wotton-under-Edge, Gloucestershire, where the owners' Rottweiler refused to enter a haunted bedroom while a ghost was present.

Apports

When a physical object or objects appear from nowhere and without any explanation. Often apports will be relevant to the spirit that delivered them and may give a clue as to its identity.

Asports

When a physical object suddenly, completely and inexplicably vamishes

Befriending Phenomena

When a ghost apparently attempts to befriend a living person. In most cases the witness is a child and the ghost is benign.

Camera Phenomena

The inexplicable effects a ghost can have on cameras. These include causing them to malfunction or the batteries to drain, blank prints to replace pictures or the film to rewind or jump out of the camera unaided. Locations where this happens regularly are said to be subject to the 'jinx factor'.

Below: *The famous direct writing that occurred at Borley Rectory in Essex was just one of a number of phenomena that affected the house, which was once considered the most haunted property in Britain. The writing is also considered to be the best example of ghost writing.*

Direct Writing Phenomena

Writing believed to be of supernatural origin and produced when a spirit temporarily possesses a medium and manipulates his or her hand to write. Occasionally, however, the writing is not produced by a human hand, and in these instances it is believed that the writing has come directly from the entity without the temporal possession of a human body. In the case of Borley Rectory in Essex, there were many examples of direct writing on the walls of the rectory, always appealing for help and a 'light mass'.

Disembodied Voices

When a witness hears the inexplicable sound of voices although no-one is present.

Displacement of Objects

The anomalous moving of objects, usually without breaking them and often at great speed. Sometimes objects are simply moved from one place to another, other times they are taken away and appear at a later date in a very obvious place.

Above: *Ghosts can be useful! Sometimes entities have been known to cause broken instruments, such as clocks, to function perfectly again (see page 26).*

Door Phenomena

The inexplicable – and purposeless – opening, closing, slamming, locking or unlocking of doors.

Below: *EMF meters are used to detect and monitor levels of electromagnetic energy, as such energy can be affected by the presence of ghosts.*

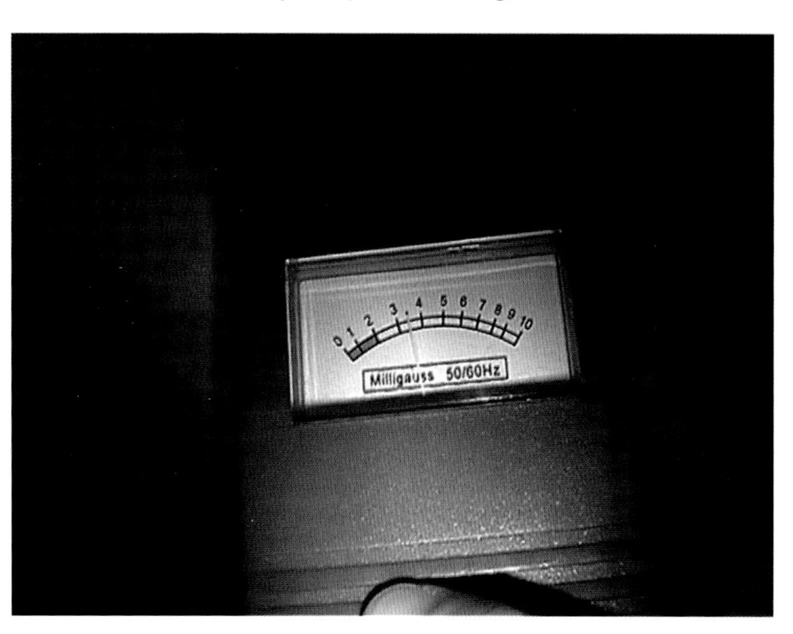

Dysfunction of Otherwise Functional Objects

When things that have been working perfectly suddenly break down but no apparent malfunction can be found when it is taken to be repaired.

Electromagnetic Variations

Inexplicable changes in the electromagnetic field, which are detected and monitored using EMF meters.

Following Phenomena

When ghosts follow people from one place to another. One famous example occurred at Ettington Park Hotel in Warwickshire – a couple 'took home' the ghosts of two children after staying at the hotel. When the couple returned to the hotel the child spirits were also returned to their former haunt.

Footfall
The sound of an invisible entity's footsteps.

Function of Otherwise Non-functional Objects
When a broken or disused object suddenly starts working perfectly again, such as an unwound clock.

Ghostprints and Ghoststeps
The effect of ghosts leaving hand- or footprints in dust, soil, chalk or flour (often used in set-up test situations).

Above: *Inexplicable or psychic breezes are often reported when ghost activity is witnessed.*

Intelligent or Random Knocking, Banging, Scratching or Rapping
The sound of knocking, banging, scratching or rapping which may be in answer to questions set for the spirit or which may occur apparently at random.

Intense Unpleasant Atmosphere
The feeling that all is not quite right. The uncomfortable sensation of being watched by something or of a brooding menace or of being unwelcome in some way.

Involuntary Temporary Possession
When a poltergeist 'takes over' the body of the witness or trigger person and speaks through their mouth. There are many examples of this, including the famous 1970s case of the Enfield poltergeist.

Levitation of Objects or People
The manipulation of objects (and in some cases people) by ghosts, so that they apparently float above ground and move around unaided.

Lithobolia
The throwing of stones that do not originate from the immediate surroundings. Often these stones are thrown with great force from the sky onto the roof of a building. In Canada these are known as 'Witch Balls'.

Manipulation of Free Energy to Power Otherwise Disconnected Electrical Equipment
When electrical equipment functions of its own accord without being connected to an electricity supply. For example, a television switching on while unplugged.

Manipulation of Time Itself to Cause Temporal Displacement
The temporary effect a haunting has on time in order that the witness of the haunting seems to move backwards or forwards in time.

Paranormal Motivation
When a ghost controls a witness without the subject being aware of what is happening.

Physical Displacement of the World as We Perceive It
A temporary change in the physical make-up of the landscape, architecture or environment while the haunting is taking place.

Physical Interaction with Physical Displacement of the World as We Perceive It
The phenomenon whereby the ghost interacts physically with something that was present in a different time. For example, when a ghost appears to be climbing an invisible staircase – a staircase that was there in the past but is no longer present.

Psychic Breezes or Wind
The anomalous occurrence of a breeze or wind that cannot come from a natural source.

Psychic Echo
A sound of ghostly origin that does not seem to originate from a single, identifiable source but instead seems to surround the witness. Feelings of unease often accompany this phenomenon.

Rattling Pictures
When a ghost rattles pictures or moves them around so that they no longer hang correctly.

Screams, Cries, Moans and Wails
The sound of a distressed spectre.

Sibilant Whisperings
The anomalous sound of voices whispering. The voices are loud enough to be heard but not clear enough to be understood.

Sound Mimicking
The occurrence of familiar sounds that do not have a source. For example, the sound of glass breaking or furniture being dragged across a floor when neither event is occurring in the immediate area.

Spectral Music
The phenomenon of a musical instrument playing itself, such as the harpsichord at Levens Hall in Cumbria, which has been clearly heard despite there being nobody playing it.

Spectral Scents
The creation of paranormal smells and scents, perhaps of food, flowers, incense, aftershave or cigars. They may be localized, stationary or mobile. They usually come and go very quickly, unlike naturally occurring smells and scents.

Spectral Singing
The sound of singing or chanting that cannot be explained and is, therefore, attributed to ghosts.

Spontaneous Combustion
The inexplicable spontaneous outbreak and extinguishing of fires by paranormal influence. The cases normally cause minimal damage and the objects affected are usually of little value to their owners. Poltergeists often adopt this kind of behaviour.

Stacking Phenomena
The strange occurrence of the stacking of household objects, such as chairs or jars, on top of one another to form a tower. Objects stacked by ghosts are often too

Above: *Pictures moving of their own accord or rattling vigorously is often a sign of ghostly activity.*

Below: *Stacking phenomena has been recorded in many cases of ghost activity, often when the haunting involves a poltergeist.*

intricately balanced for humans to copy the feat.

Tactual Phenomena
The sensation of a ghost pushing, stroking, touching, kicking or even trying to strangle the witness.

Telephone Phenomena
Any inexplicable activity surrounding a telephone. In particular, telephones ringing despite being disconnected. More spectacularly, there are examples of ghosts ringing people in the living world and having conversations with them. In instances such as these, the ghost is normally calling to say goodbye to the witness.

Temperature Variations
The experience of rapid and extreme temperature changes for no logical reason. The temperature change is always localized, intense and instant. On one particular occasion that I was witness to, the temperature dropped so low it was akin to standing in a freezer and I could actually see my breath.

Temporary Witness Paralysis
When ghosts frighten witnesses to the extent that they become temporarily paralyzed.

Throwing of Objects
The phenomenon whereby objects are thrown around by an unseen force.

Water Phenomena
The inexplicable manifestation of water, especially perfect circles of water, often delivered by poltergeists.
Each of the seven ghost categories is set out below with its known phenomena profiles and details of occurrences of each type of ghost in its category.

Some Unexpected Facts About Ghosts

- There are more recorded experiences of ghosts and sightings of apparitions in Great Britain than in any other country in the world.
- Eighty-four per cent of ghost sightings are witnessed during daylight hours.
- In the 1960s, it was recorded that there were over 10,000 haunted locations in England, Scotland and Wales. Although this number has risen since then, it is worth remembering that this statistic *only* includes ghosts that have been reported. There may be many thousands more witnessed but not reported. There may also be many witnesses who do not realize that what they are experiencing or seeing is a ghost.
- One person in ten will see a ghost in their lifetime, although not all will know they are witnessing a ghost.
- Children under ten are more likely to see ghosts than older children or adults.
- There are more recorded sightings of ghosts on 31 October (Hallowe'en) than on any other day of the year. A possible explanation for this could be that people expect to see spectres on that day and are, therefore, more aware of paranormal activity that may otherwise have gone unnoticed.

GENERIC GHOST GROUPS

ONCE-SENTIENT GHOSTS

Afrit
This is the ghost of a murdered Arabian. The spirit rises from the blood spilt during its death as smoke rises from a fire. However, the spirit can be stopped by 'nailing down the Afrit' – driving a nail into the spilt blood.

Baka
These Haitian ghosts are said to be spirits who return after death with the intention of eating human flesh!

Bedroom Intruder
This spectre seems to manifest itself late at night. In most cases it sits on the end of the witness's bed, its ghostly weight causing the mattress to be depressed. An example of a Bedroom Intruder haunting exists at the Bull's Head inn in Inkberrow, Worcestershire, where the ghost is that of a woman.

Cauld Lad
This strange spirit has been seen repeatedly in the Durham area. It interferes in the lives of the living by creating a mess in kitchens and generally untidying houses, much like a poltergeist. The Cauld Lad is alleged to be the restless ghost of Roger Skelton, a stable boy who was murdered in 1609 by Robert Hilton, the then owner of local Hylton Castle.

Cavalier Human Figure
This is a frequently reported sighting and you don't have to visit many haunted houses before you come across this type of ghost. A good example of Cavalier Human Figures are the apparitions who fight a duel at Athelhampton Hall in Dorset.

Church Grim
This is the animal equivalent of a Graveyard Guardian (see page 31). In English folklore, it is written that, traditionally, a large black dog was slain and buried in a new graveyard to be its guardian and to protect future residents from evil presences. Other accounts name this phantom Kirk Grim and describe it as an animal phantom of a lamb, a horse or a pig. In Cornwall, this spectre is referred to as a Kergrim.

Dismembered Figures, Incorporeal Heads and Partial Figures
These gruesome manifestations are alarmingly common. These hauntings always appear as dismembered parts of the human anatomy, such as the head and shoulders that glides down a gallery at Chicksands Priory in Bedfordshire. Others, such as those called 'incorporeal heads', appear to simply float around on their own without any sign of a body.

One explanation for the occurrence of partial figures is that they lack the energy necessary for total

Below: *A cauld lad haunts Hylton Castle in County Durham, where he makes mischief by untidying various rooms of the ancient property.*

Above: *Phantoms of monks and nuns are commonly reported in the vicinity of abbeys, churches and vicarages.*

materialization. Another reason is the simple fact that the ghost's limb was deliberately separated from its body in life. A good photographic example of a partial-figure apparition was caught on film in the library at Combermere Abbey, Shropshire, on 5 December 1891.

Ecclesiastical Human Figures

As with Human Figures of Indistinct Appearance (see page 33), these holy hauntings are some of the most common in the British Isles. Almost every monastery, ruined cathedral, abbey or vicarage has at some time experienced supernatural activity. Although many ghosts appear to be monks or nuns they may, in fact, have been other types of ghost, such as medieval knights, or actors dressed for a performance. Hence it is vital that ghost hunters keep an open mind about what they have seen and do not jump to conclusions or make assumptions.

Family Ghosts

Some families have their own ghosts, which sometimes stay with them for hundreds of years. These ghosts are often attached to the families of titled people, such as earls or lords. Possibly this is because, in the past, families with enormous power were able to commit terrible crimes without ever being brought to justice. Many family ghosts appear as portents of death for other family members; others appear in times of trouble.

In Denmark, one particular family ghost appears as an eerie shadow of a gallows with a body hanging from it just before a family death. This haunting began over 150 years ago and is said to have started after an ancestor was wrongfully hanged. There are other types of Never-Sentient Family Ghosts, and these are listed in the Elemental Ghosts section (see pages 44–52).

Another family ghost is similar in appearance to St Elmo's Fire (see page 50) and is known as Vingoe Fire because it haunts the Vingoe family of Cornwall. This elemental entity appears as small flame-like lights and foretells the death of a family member.

Gallows Ghosts

Gallows Ghosts are found, not surprisingly, at sites where gallows once stood. During the Middle Ages, gallows were built at crossroads in order to confuse any ghost returning to avenge its death as to which road to take and thereby render the ghost unable to find the people who condemned it to die.

One example of a Gallows Ghost haunting takes place in a shop in Cornwall. The building stands on the site of an old gallows and the ghost is seen in the shop, sometimes appearing on the security camera. Gallows Ghosts seem to be unable to leave the site of the gallows they died upon.

Ghost Animals

Ghosts of animals are just as common as the human variety, and as many different ghost animals have been experienced as you can think of. I was once given an account of a sighting of a mouse's ghost that disappeared. The most common ghost animals are those of domestic pets, such as cats and dogs. My mother once saw the ghost of her childhood cat in the house that they once shared.

Ghost Birds

These are less common than ghost animals but are not unheard of. One such haunting takes place at Wallington, near Belsay in Northumberland. Here, the sound of many birds beating their wings against the windows

has often been witnessed. The phenomenon is sometimes accompanied by the sound of heavy breathing.

Other examples of bird hauntings include the White Bird of Oxenham Manor in Devon, which ominously appears when a member of the family is about to die.

Graveyard Guardians

It is a general misconception that graveyards are full of ghosts, but this is not usually the case. Ghosts tend to haunt the place of their death, or a place they had a strong connection with, and neither of these is often a graveyard. Graveyards always have one ghost, however, and that is the ghost of the first person to be buried there.

In Western Europe there was an ancient ritual that a living person had to be sacrificed when a new burial ground was established in order to insure that it would have a Graveyard Guardian. It is the job of the Guardian to ward off evil spirits and unwanted intruders. Photographs taken in graveyards, particularly at night, often show supernatural anomalies and these may be the energy of the Graveyard Guardian. In Europe, these are called 'Ankou'.

Above: *Legend has it that the first burial in a newly consecrated graveyard will rise from the dead and become that graveyard's guardian.*

Green Jean

Similar to England's 'White Lady' ghosts, the Scottish Highlands are home to many variations of 'Green Jean' ghosts. They tend to haunt isolated castles, manor houses and lonely glens and they appear as female figures with either green apparel or a ghostly green glow.

One well-known Green Jean haunts Ashintully Castle near Pitlochry. Here, so the story goes, the lady of the castle – named Jean – was murdered by her uncle because he was jealous of her position. He cut her throat and was then obliged to murder her maid for fear she would discover his dark deeds. The uncle stuffed the body of the maid up the chimney and dragged Jean's body down the stairs. Her ghost can now be glimpsed on moonlit nights standing next to the headstone that her uncle erected in her memory. She was murdered in a green dress – which is why she now appears as a Green Jean ghost.

Above: *Phantom appearances of witches are rare, although they have been reported at Treryn Dinas in Cornwall.*

Grey Ladies

Grey Ladies appear everywhere! Hundreds of sites claim to have them. Bearing in mind what was said about Ecclesiastical Human Figures, it is important to remember that a lot of Grey Ladies will turn out to be a different sort of ghost when investigated more closely.

Hag/Witch

Ghosts of witches and hags are rarely reported, possibly because they look similar to Grey Ladies. There are, however, some genuine reports of witch ghosts, one of which was at Treryn Dinas in Cornwall. Here, a coven of witch ghosts were sighted dancing round a bubbling cauldron and cackling loudly.

Headless Horseman

Headless riders have been reported along many a country lane, and one such ghost haunts the lanes of the site of Knighton Gorges, a now-derelict haunted mansion on the Isle of Wight. Other examples of this type of ghost have also been reported in German and Scandinavian folklore.

Headless Human Figure

This is the traditional English country house ghost and it often appears headless, carrying his or her head under its arm. Such ghosts sometimes appear headless because they were beheaded, but not in all cases, so the reason for some being decapitated is unknown.

One intriguing headless ghost materializes in Longridge in Lancashire, where it will accompany you as you walk along the road, only revealing itself as a ghost when it turns to face you and you are confronted with an empty hood. It's a ghost with a sordid sense of humour, because it then proceeds to open its basket, out of which jumps its head; the head then chases the witness away to the sound of maniacal mocking laughter. Certainly not your usual headless haunting!

Historically Important or Royal Human Figures

Sightings of historical and royal ghosts are well documented. They are commonly reported because they are recognizable: for example, the ghost of Sir Francis Drake (*c.* 1540–1596) is witnessed in several locations, including the Ship Inn in Exeter, Devon. These hauntings are also commonly reported because people assume that if a ghost appears somewhere that is associated with a famous person, then it must be the spirit of that personage. However, this isn't always the case.

Human Figure on Horseback

This may appear as a soldier, a cavalier, a Roman, etc. or it may appear as a present-day rider. The horse itself is part of the ghostly apparition but as a human figure is seen astride it, it is still classed as a Human Figure on Horseback.

A famous haunting of this type has been witnessed at Cranborne Chase near Old Sarum in Wiltshire, where a Bronze Age horseman has been seen on several occasions.

Human Figure that is Identifiable as a Previous Occupant of a Location

Exactly the same as a Human Figure of Indistinct Appearance except that in this instance the witness

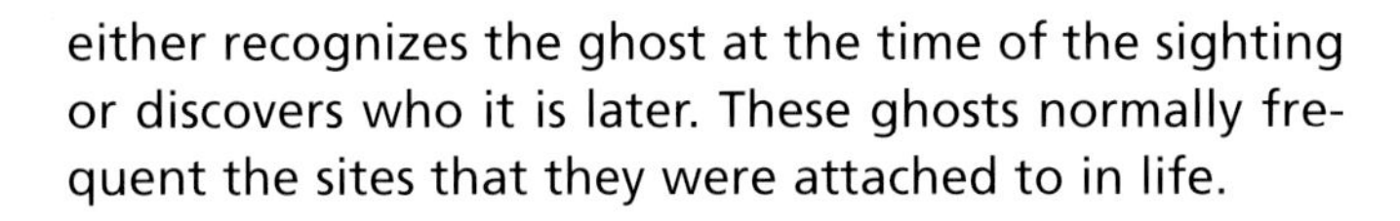

either recognizes the ghost at the time of the sighting or discovers who it is later. These ghosts normally frequent the sites that they were attached to in life.

Below: *Old Cornish tin mines are sometimes inhabited by helpful spirits known as Knockers.*

Human Figure of Indistinct Appearance

Perhaps the most common of all ghosts are the mundane spectres that look almost identical to any stranger on the street, until they disappear!

These phenomena have no particular visual features to indicate that they are ghosts. They may be linked to the location at which they appear or they may be 'passing through' along ley lines or ghost paths or they may be attached to a person or object.

Incubus

Those unfortunate enough to encounter an Incubus find themselves interacting sexually with a presence. In some cases the incubus will be visible, but in others only the sensations and physical force of the sexual interaction will be experienced. Incubi are apparently male and interact with living females. Accounts of visible post-sentient Incubi describe them as attractive human males. Why these ghosts return to sexually attack people is unknown.

Innocence Ghost

In Cornwall, women who are seduced and deserted by their lovers and die either through childbirth or disgrace are renowned for returning as Innocence Ghosts. They not only haunt their seducer but also his family – and for several generations afterwards, too.

Invisibles

This is a term coined to describe invisible 'playmates' of young children. Often the playmate is a ghost, and not a figment of the child's imagination as is commonly believed.

Knockers

Knockers are the ghosts of the Jews who were involved in the crucifixion of Christ and were sent as slaves by the Romans to work in the mines of Cornwall. They are unique to Cornwall and are said to knock on the walls to show the miners where to dig. Their ghostly knocking gets louder and more impatient as the miners get closer to the minerals. Upsetting Knockers is considered very dangerous and offerings of food are always left for them.

Kobold

These cunning spirits are evil and malicious. They dwell in mines,

Above: *Ghosts of children often befriend their living counterparts, and they are sometimes confused with imaginary friends by adults.*

Popstar **Sting** and his wife **Trudie Styler** fled their luxury London mansion after living there for just 18 months. The house was haunted by a woman and child, who appeared along with a cold chill in their bedroom. But that was nothing compared to the carving knife that was thrown by an unseen power across the kitchen with such force that it embedded itself in the far wall.

where they cause rockfalls and other accidents so that the miners cannot work.

Lemure
Roman ghosts who return to haunt their descendants and families are known as lemures and their intent is always evil. Lemures are sensitive to sound, so only loud noise will scare them away. In order to prevent hauntings, the Romans used to burn black beans around the tomb of anyone whom they thought may become a Lemure – it was thought that the stench was so bad no spirit would wish to cross through the fetid smoke.

Liekkio
This Finnish spectre is similar in appearance to Britain's Will-o'-the-Wisp and appears as a dancing flame where a death is imminent. The spirits are said to be those of the souls of children who have been buried in unmarked graves.

Old Bloody Bones
Known to haunt the area around Baldhu in Cornwall, this spectre is a remnant of a terrible battle that took place here. Its appearance is thin and waif-like and is dripping with the blood of its open battle wounds.

Period Human Figures of Any Era
These stately spectres drift around historic halls, castles and houses. They are often **oblivious** ghosts and can be found at many ancient sites. The Victorian, Edwardian, Georgian, Elizabethan, Tudor and medieval eras have all produced countless hauntings.

Phantom Battle
These are easily confused with Timeslips, but they are classed as Phantom Battles because they were once sentient, which is not the case with all Timeslips. These hauntings are often **cyclic** and always **oblivious**. Phantom battles seem to re-enact themselves over and over again, although with some degree of variation, so they are not always witnessed in the same way.

The most famous examples of Phantom Battles take place on Marston Moor in Yorkshire and at Edgehill in Warwickshire.

Phantom Children
Children are among the most commonly reported ghosts and are often seen by living children, who in many cases unknowingly adopt them as playmates.

At Chingle Hall in Lancashire, however, the ghost of a little girl in a yellow dress has been seen crossing a

drawbridge (now a stone bridge) by an adult rather than by a child. Other phantom children have been seen at Chingle Hall, too: once a group were seen dancing round a tree in the grounds by a living child who got most upset when her mother said she could not see the little girls that she was asking to play with. A ghostly boy is also resident here; he appeared in a photograph taken of a grandfather clock.

Phantom Drummers

Ghostly drummers are found in various castles in the British Isles and they are exactly what their name suggests. These ghoulish musicians parade their haunting-ground, incessantly drumming as they go. The reasons for the drumming is different from case to case.

A good example haunts Herstmonceux Castle in Sussex where the drummer is a giant and even has a room named after him – The Drummers Hall.

Phantom Hitch-hiker

These come into the common categories of ghost types. There are many stories of these strange ghosts, which seem to be quite human to the witness until they suddenly vanish. Phantom hitch-hikers stand on the sides of roads trying to hitch a lift from passing cars. Once a car stops, they get in and occasionally even strike up a conversation with the driver. After a short time the ghost completely vanishes leaving the driver shaken and confused by the experience.

Above: *Longleat House in Wiltshire is haunted by a phantom lady that is thought to be the spirit of Lady Louisa Carteret.*

Phantom Ladies

These are relatively common hauntings in Britain, and these ghosts are often referred to as a generic colour even when they are known individuals. For example, Longleat House in Wiltshire has a famous Green Lady although she has been identified as the phantom of Lady Louise Carteret. At The Ancient Ram Inn in Gloucestershire the phantom lady is pink, while at Stirling Castle, Stirlingshire, she is red so Phantom Ladies can appear in many colours. In the north of England and on the borders, ghosts of white ladies are sometimes referred to as a 'Silkie' or 'Silky' – in these cases though the ghosts are said to terrorize lazy servants and help with household chores!

Phantom Traveller

These ghosts appear in your car while you are driving along and vanish after a short time. They are sometimes glimpsed in the mirror sitting behind you on the back seat. They are similar to phantom hitch-hikers, except that they simply appear in your car without first asking for a lift!

Above: *At Bluebell Hill in Kent, 43 people have witnessed a run over re-enactment since 1934.*

Radiant Boys

Accounts of these glowing ghosts are found all over the world. They take the form of beautiful male children who materialize surrounded by a figure-hugging aura of brilliant unnatural light. Radiant boys seem to occur in different colours but are primarily blue or white. Chillingham Castle in Northumberland has a blue radiant boy, while Corby Castle in Cumbria has a white one.

Who they are or why they haunt is unknown, but a popular belief suggests that they are the ghosts of children who have been murdered by their parents. Although it is not always the case, it has become generally accepted that seeing a Radiant Boy is a warning of misfortune for the witness.

Revenant

This type of ghost returns to haunt for a particular reason. It has unfinished business and cannot rest until some sort of action is completed or a wrong is put right. In short, a revenant is a ghost with a purpose. Revenant hauntings usually cease when their business is completed.

Roman Human Figures

Since the Romans occupied the British Isles in 43–410 AD, many ghosts from that time have been reported. They are sometimes **oblivious** and can be found perambulating around Roman remains.

One famous example of a Roman haunting is that which takes place on the City Walls of Chester, where a lone Roman centurion has been seen.

Run Over Re-enactment

These are always **reactive** and **conscious** and are often startling. These ghosts re-enact their own deaths by appearing in the path of cars on certain stretches of road up and down the country. They are not timeslips because the surrounding landscape does not alter during the experience.

Some re-enactments are actually hit by real cars. Drivers have reported hearing and feeling the thump as they hit the ghost, at which point they slam on the brakes and get out to find the victim, only to find that there is nobody there.

One example of a haunting of this type occurs on the Stocksbridge Bypass, near Sheffield. Another centres on Blue Bell Hill in Kent, where the ghost of a young woman in white has been 'run-over' by 43 witnesses since 1934.

Screaming Skulls

These are found in numerous houses up and down the British Isles. Each case is slightly different, but in all instances the hauntings are **reactive**: they do nothing until the skull involved is affected in some way that it objects to.

Skulls of this sort have been known to affect crops, cause diseases or produce screams whenever they are moved from the building in which they reside. The disturbances cease only when the skull is returned to its home, at which point the haunting becomes dormant again.

There are many screaming skull hauntings. Wardley Hall in Manchester has been so badly affected in the past that the tenancy of the skull is now written into the lease of the building!

Shadow Forms or Figures

These are indistinct and look like an ordinary person's shadow, except that there is nothing to cast the shadow in reality. Shadow forms, or 'wraiths' as they are often called, are common hauntings. The shadow that haunts Harlaxton Manor in Grantham, Lincolnshire, resides in the 'haunted bedroom'.

Spunkie

In Scottish folklore, spunkies are the unhappy spirits of unbaptized children who haunt both land and sea, continually looking for someone who will name them. Reports tell of spunkies grouping together for comfort. West Country legend also tells of these sad souls, but here they can turn into white moths and flit unnoticed among the living. On All Hallows Eve (Hallowe'en), spunkies are said to gather at graveyards to meet the ghosts of those who have recently departed.

Succubus

A succubus is the female version of an incubus. Succubi are often described as beautiful voluptuous women and they interact sexually with living men. All accounts of incubus and succubus encounters have taken place at night.

An example of a well-documented case of this type of haunting occurs at The Ancient Ram Inn in Wotton-under-Edge, Gloucestershire, where the owner tells me he has been the victim of the succubus' presence. He recalls physically wrestling the 'thing' off him as it was an extremely strong and muscular entity. He also stated that he thinks it was a male incubus on that particular occasion, which suggest that these ghosts can have multiple sexual orientations.

Trickster Spirit

The ghosts of Native American Indians killed during the Seminole Wars of 1858 haunt the Everglades of Florida in the United States. They take revenge on the white men who killed them by appearing as dancing lights and luring them to watery graves in the treacherous swamplands.

Undine

These are the lovelorn spectres of women who have drowned themselves after a failed love affair. Their sad spirits float among waters and hide in trees, harmless to all but their cold-hearted lovers.

Utukku

This is an Assyrian spirit of evil intent.

Below: *Undines hide among leafy treetops or in watery graves across Britain and Europe.*

Phenomena Caused by Once-Sentient Ghosts

- Animal Phenomena
- Apports
- Asports
- Befriending Phenomena
- Camera Phenomena
- Direct Writing Phenomena
- Disembodied Voices
- Displacement of Objects
- Door Phenomena
- Dysfunction of Otherwise Functional Objects
- Electromagnetic Variations
- Following Phenomena
- Footfall
- Ghostprints and Ghoststeps
- Intelligent or random Knocking, Banging, Scratching or Rapping
- Intense Unpleasant Atmosphere
- Involuntary Temporary Possession
- Levitation of Objects or People
- Manipulation of Free Energy to Power Otherwise Disconnected Electrical Equipment
- Paranormal Motivation
- Psychic Breezes or Wind
- Psychic Echo
- Screams, Cries, Moans or Wails
- Sibilant Whisperings
- Soectral Music
- Spectral Scents
- Spectral Singing
- Spontaneous Combustion
- Temporary Witness Paralysis
- Throwing of Objects
- Rattling Pictures
- Tactual Phenomena
- Telephone Phenomena
- Temperature Variations

Vacant Painting Haunting

These are relatively rare and can only occur where there is a painting of the ghost, as the ghost haunts the building in which it led its sentient life. The person depicted in the painting steps out when the ghost walks, leaving the painting empty, and only returns to the picture when the its perambulations are complete.

One example of this kind of haunting takes place at Bisham Abbey in Berkshire, and it was last witnessed in 1910.

Wall-walkers

These spectral visitors pass through the walls of buildings that have since been built on a route that they may have followed during their sentient life. Wall-walkers are oblivious to their physical surroundings. It is important to remember that not all Once-Sentient Ghosts follow this pattern, as many seem to adjust to alterations that have taken place since their death.

One example of a wall-walker exists at Marlberry Cottage in Swanage, Dorset, where the resident ghost passes through the wall on the exact spot where there is a bricked-up door.

Wartime Human Figures

Not surprisingly, due to the high number of fatalities, wartime ghosts are reported from many eras.

INANIMATE GHOSTS

Coach & Horses (With or Without Horseman)

The most famous phantom coach and horses in Britain is the one used by a nun and monk from Essex's Borley Rectory case – they allegedly fled the village in order to continue their secret love affair. Another coach and horses haunts the Kentish village of Pluckley.

Ghost Planes

There are many accounts of Ghost Planes from all over the world, and most seem to be the result of tragic air crashes. Longdendale Valley in Derbyshire seems to be where they are most prevalent in Britain. Iindeed, there are many crash sites here and the wreckage of Second World War Bombers can still be found on the moors. When sighted, the ghost planes seem to soar silently in the sky and then disappear inexplicably from view. Some re-enact their fatal crashes complete with sound.

Above: *The spectacular spectral ship the* Lady Lovibond *re-enacts its mid-18th-century demise on Goodwin Sands in Kent every 50 years.*

Ghost Ships

Stories of ghostly galleons sailing the high seas were frequently the topic of mariners' tales in the 18th century, and even today there are accounts of similar hauntings. *The Flying Dutchman* has been seen many times around the Cape of Good Hope, sailing its spectral course through the skies, above the stormy seas. Accounts of its appearances have even been recorded by the British Admiralty. *The Lady Lovibond* is another spectral ship whose anniversary haunting re-enacts its demise on Goodwin Sands in Kent on 13 February every 50 years.

Ghost Submarines

Accounts of this type of haunting are rare, but there is one particularly fine example. The submarine was the UB65, which was built in 1916 for use during the First World War (1914–18). From its initial construction it was plagued with suicides and peculiar fatal accidents among those who built it and those assigned as crew. One account tells of a ghostly green glow filling the hull and of the general functions of the craft behaving out of character. A ghost of a lieutenant was also sighted standing on the outer rim of the bulk on several occasions. Abandoned by its crew, it made its last appearance late on in the war before slipping beneath the waves for the last time, taking its lost souls with it.

Ghost Trains

Accounts of Ghost Trains tell of ghostly carriages and engines pulling silently into stations where no track remains. One such account is told of United States' President Abraham Lincoln's (1809–65) funeral train, which is seen in phantom form on 27 April each year, retracing its journey between Washington and Illinois.

Ghost Vehicles

Ghostly appearances of mechanized transport are common and include sightings of cars, taxis, bicycles and even buses. London is noted as having a famous bus haunting in Kensington, which was once seen frequently by local residents, garage owners and motorists – some of whom swerved to avoid crashing with it only to see it disappear in front of their very eyes.

Haunted Objects

Accounts of haunted objects can be found all over the world, but how or why an object becomes haunted varies. They are assumed to have no soul or personality of their own (having never been sentient). Haunted objects do things that would normally be impossible. The most frequently haunted objects are clocks, chairs, beds and paintings. Clocks in particular can act peculiarly when their owner dies. In one account a clock stopped at the exact time its owner passed over to the other side, only to start working again on being wound. It stopped again the next night at the same time as the night before. It started again each time it was wound but stopped at the same time as its owner's death every day until his body was buried. It then worked perfectly again until the anniversary of his death a year later. It continued this ghostly anniversary for ten years, afterwards working perfectly.

Phenomena Caused by Inanimate Ghosts

- Animal Phenomena
- Apports
- Asports
- Camera Phenomena
- Dysfunction of Otherwise Functional Objects
- Electromagnetic Variations
- Function of Otherwise Non-functional Objects
- Intense Unpleasant Atmosphere
- Levitation of Objects and People
- Manipulation of Free Energy to Power Otherwise Disconnected Electrical Equipment
- Musical Instrument Phenomena
- Psychic Breezes or Wind
- Psychic Echo
- Temperature Variations

Below: *Longdendale Valley in Derbyshire is frequently haunted by the ghost planes of bombers that crashed here during the Second World War (1939–45).*

POLTERGEISTS

Above: *In Russia, noisy poltergeists are known as Domovoys, but they can be very useful as they perform household chores!*

Domovoy
This is a noisy Russian spirit that performs household chores and disturbs the residents by making loud noises.

Mumiai
This Indian poltergeist is known for throwing objects about and attacking people. Never revealing itself, it delights in focusing its paranormal attention on those who are lazy or who have criminal tendencies.

Location-based Poltergeist
The word poltergeist is German for 'noisy ghost'. It is now an accepted term used to describe several kinds of key phenomena – namely, movement of objects and noises. Location-based poltergeist infestations are closely linked to specific sites and draw energy to create phenomena from various sources. An example of a location-based poltergeist is at Sizergh Castle in Cumbria, where the phenomena are not centred on an individual, but on the very castle itself.

Person-based Poltergeist
This is a more common form of poltergeist. It centres on a specific person whose presence induces the entity to perform. In many cases, the focus of the poltergeist's attention is a young female. It has been suggested that the telekinetic energy of pubescent girls is dramatically higher than that of boys, which is why the poltergeist chooses to latch onto these 'victims'. The most famous account of this type of haunting occurred in Enfield in London during the 1970s.

Phenomena Caused by Poltergeists

- Apports
- Asports
- Befriending Phenomena
- Camera Phenomena
- Direct Writing Phenomena
- Disembodied Voices
- Displacement of Objects
- Door Phenomena
- Electromagnetic Variations
- Footfall
- Intelligent or Random Knocking, Banging, Scratching or Rapping
- Involuntary Temporary Possession
- Levitation of Objects or People
- Lithobolia
- Manipulation of Free Energy to Power Otherwise Disconnected Electrical Equipment
- Psychic Breezes or Wind
- Screams, Cries, Moans or Wails
- Sound Mimicking
- Spectral Scents
- Spectral Singing
- Spontaneous Combustion
- Stacking Phenomena
- Tactual Phenomena
- Temperature Variations
- Throwing of Objects
- Water Phenomena

Phenomena Caused by Doppelgängers

- Animal Phenomena
- Camera Phenomena
- Disembodied Voices
- Spectral Music
- Spectral Singing
- Temperature Variations

DOPPELGÄNGERS (ALSO KNOWN AS FETCHES AND WRAITHS)

Animal Doppelgänger

These are the same as Human Doppelgängers (see below) except they mimic animals rather than humans.

Human Doppelgänger

These are among the strangest ghost encounters reported. Doppelgängers actually take on the physical appearance of someone living. When witnesses see them, they do not realize anything odd is occurring until afterwards when they discover that the 'person' seen could not possibly have been in that location at that time. Why these spirits choose this behaviour is unknown. In Scotland they are known as 'Co-Walkers' and have a tendency to appear at funerals – terrifying anyone who sees them.

There are many cases of human doppelgängers in my archives, and one example involved myself many years ago. A friend of mine 'saw' me and my father drive past him in our family car. I was due to meet this friend shortly afterwards and when I didn't appear he called my mobile phone to see where I was going in the car, only to have me answer the phone from my home as I had not yet left the house that day!

Another form of human doppelgänger is known as a Crisis Apparition. This term has been accepted as a means of explaining phantoms that appear to the witness at a time of grave danger. The doppelgänger takes the form of the person in danger and presents itself as a spectral message to a witness to warn them that the person it resembles is in a crisis situation. Reports of these phenomena are commonplace.

Inanimate Doppelgänger

These have never been sentient and yet are witnessed. They include doppelgänger cars, as in the example featured in Human Doppelgänger above.

TIMESLIP GHOSTS (ALSO KNOWN AS 'PLACE MEMORY')

Immersion Timeslip

Timeslip ghost experiences are rare, but are, without doubt, the most bizarre and fascinating paranormal encounter you could possibly have. During the experience the percipient is apparently completely immersed in another period of time. The era they are transported to is normally the past – but not always, for there are examples of timeslips from the future. During the experience, the witness is able to interact with the environment physically.

The most famous account of this experience was when two elderly ladies visited the Palace of Versailles in France on 10 August 1901. Here, they were privileged to see a ghostly vision of the palace as it used to be and the spectre of Marie Antoinette.

Phantom Battle

Spectral re-enactments of highly charged wartime scenes have been reported throughout the world. They range from sounds to full paranormal spectacles, either on the ground or in some cases in the skies above the battle scene. They are usually **anniversary** appearances. A famous case of this phenomenon is found at Gettysburg in Pennsylvania, USA, where one of the most famous battles of the American Civil War (1861–5) took place in July 1863.

Phantom Bells

The sound of bells ringing from churches that have since been submerged beneath the sea or lakes is a phenomenon that has been reported all over the British Isles. It is a timeslip haunting that has been witnessed at such places as Dunwich in Suffolk and

Lyonnesse in Cornwall. They seem to favour Christmas as a time to toll, and people have noticed that they also seem to warn of approaching storms.

Above: *Battlefields, such as those of the American Civil War (1861–5), are often haunted by phantom battles for many years after the event.*

Phantom Buildings

Phantom Buildings take many forms and appear to be the actual ghosts of buildings. Their manifestation is often accompanied by secondary effects, such as a feeling of intense unease or a chill in the air. One example took place in Wallington in Surrey in 1968. A Mr Chase was waiting for his bus to arrive when he noticed two small cottages with thatched roofs and pretty gardens. A plaque reading '1837' was attached on the wall of one cottage. When he returned later, they were gone and in their place stood two brick houses. Research proved that there had been two thatched cottages on that site, but they had been demolished many years earlier.

Phantom Funeral Cortège

These are always **oblivious** and take the form of a procession of ghostly undertakers carrying a coffin, or a coffin inside a hearse. One famous account of this phenomenona comes from Lyme Park in Cheshire, where a procession is occasionally seen making its way towards a small hill, known as Knight's Low. It is believed to be the phantom re-enactment of the funeral cortège of Sir Piers Legh, who died in Paris in 1422. His body was brought back to Cheshire to be buried, and it is said to have rested for a short while on Knight's Low.

Phenomena Caused by Timeslip Ghosts

- Animal Phenomena
- Camera Phenomena
- Disembodied Voices
- Footfall
- Intense Unpleasant Atmosphere
- Manipulation of Time Itself to Cause Temporal Displacement of Time.
- Physical Displacement of the World As We Perceive It
- Physical Interaction with Physical Displacement of the World as we Perceive It
- Psychic Breezes or Wind
- Psychic Echo
- Screams, Cries, Moans and Wails
- Spectral Music
- Spectral Scents
- Spectral Singing
- Temperature Variations

Above: *Found all over Ireland, the banshee is a screaming phantom whose wailing heralds death.*

ELEMENTAL GHOSTS

Elemental ghosts are frightening phantoms that envelop those who experience them with a powerful force. These ghosts, which usually attach themselves to specific sites or buildings, are so horrifying that their very presence can induce an overwhelming sense of evil and fear. Born out of turbulent or depraved actions, they form an entity of combined evil from numerous events. Elementals are among the most primitive of all ghosts, and their manifestation occurs mainly in rural areas. They are often **malevolent**, terrifying and unpredictable.

Alu
These hideous Assyrian hauntings appear with limbs missing and give their victims a cold, clammy embrace.

Banshee
The Banshee or, more correctly, Bean'si is an ancient Irish family haunting. It takes the form of a wailing woman whose screams and cries are heard prior to the death of a family member. In Welsh families these ghosts are called 'Death Sound' or 'Cyhyraeth', and they take the form of disembodied wailing or moaning.

Bergmonck
These ghosts haunt the treasure mines of Germany, taking on the form of gigantic robed figures.

Blue Cap
Appearing as a blue flame, these spectral helpers will aid miners in their work if offered gifts. But if they are not treated with respect they have the power to bring disaster to the mine they haunt.

Boggart
These mischievous and sometimes unpleasant ghosts are rife in northern England, where they have been known to crawl into bedrooms during the night and put their clammy hands on sleepers' faces before whipping away the bedclothes!

Bogie
These small black hairy spirits delight in tormenting and frightening the living. It is these ghosts that are referred to in the saying 'The Bogie-man will get you!'

Bull Beggar
Similar to the Galley Beggar (see page 46), but sighted in Surrey. This skeletal spectre travels by leaping from one place to the next.

Chagrin
Also known as a Congrino or Harginn. When gypsies see these ghosts they take them to be an omen of impending disaster. Chagrins appear in the form of large yellow hedgehogs.

Corpse Bird
This peculiar Welsh phantom is locally known as 'Deryn Corph'. It is a frightening phantom bird that manifests in the presence of someone as an omen of death. It usually appears at the window of the soon-to-be-deceased, tapping harshly against the glass.

Corpse Candles

The 'Canhywallan Cyrth', as it is known in its native Wales, is perhaps the most famous Welsh ghost. Corpse candles derive their name from their strange manifestation as blue or white lights strongly resembling the flames of candles. A sighting of corpse candles foretells death in the vicinity of their appearance and the colour and size of the candles indicates who is about to die: small pale blue lights for a child; large and ruddy lights for an adult; white for a woman and red for a man. Large blue, white or red flames foretell the death of one who is old and has been ill for some time.

Created Elemental Ghost

Research has suggested that it is possible to 'create' a ghost using the mind. In the early 1970s, the Toronto Society For Psychical Research designed a fictional ghost called Philip and then, after mentally 'creating' its existence, tried to contact it through séances and ouija board sessions. The results were positive, which means that they either achieved their aim or another spirit pretended to be their invented ghost.

Duppy

A West Indian ghost summoned up through a secret ritual to work at the caller's bidding. Any mortal who touches the duppy will suffer a terrible fit, and those who come into contact with its breath will be violently ill.

Ekimmu

A commonly reported Assyrian spectre that appears outside houses to give warning of approaching death by wailing incessantly.

Elemental Incubus

This entity is the same as Incubus of Once-Sentient Ghosts (see page 33), except that it is an elemental version. This means that it has never been sentient and that it is formed of energy rather than being the spirit of a departed soul.

Elemental Succubus

This entity is the same as Succubus of Once-Sentient Ghosts (see page 37), except that it is an elemental version. This means that it has never been sentient and that it is formed of energy rather than being the spirit of a departed soul.

Faery Dog

These Scottish phantoms are seen in the Highlands and Islands of Scotland. Faery Dogs are green and about the size of a small cow. They have short tails and large feet and leave paw-prints wherever they go. The Faery Dog barks loudly and clamorously three times, so anyone who hears it has the chance to seek refuge before the final, fatal bark is heard. On the Isle of Tiree there is a cavern known as 'the lair of the Faery Dog', where the barking of a dog can often be heard.

Above: *The remnants of desolate Pennard Castle in South Wales are the haunt of a Gwrach-y-rhibyn, otherwise known as a Hag of the Dribble (see page 47).*

Flapper

The Flapper is a large black creature, which morphs itself into a dark, cloaked and hooded figure with a blank face. It has been reported in rural parts of the West Country and is known to pursue anyone who sees it, flapping noisily as it follows them.

Fossegrim
The fossegrim is a spirit of the river that appears in the form of a youth playing a harp while sitting in the middle of the water. Fossegrims are quite harmless water hauntings.

Galley Beggar
This ancient spectre was first recorded in 1584. Its appearance is alarming, as it is skeleton-like with very little flesh remaining on its bones. It haunts rural areas and lanes, mostly in northern England, and gets its name from the ancient word 'gally', which means 'to frighten' or 'scare'. It also has the ability to be headless if it desires.

The most famous account of a galley beggar comes from a sighting on a hill between Over and Nether Stowey in Somerset. Here, it careers about on a toboggan with its head beneath its arm shrieking with laughter!

Ghoul
Commonly associated with stories of horror, ghouls are actually a type of Arabian ghost. They invariably haunt burial sites, where they appear in humanoid form with hideous faces and steal and feed on corpses. Sightings of ghouls range from India to Africa, and it has even been reported that they prey on travellers who are unlucky enough to fall ill while crossing deserts.

Ghostly Mist or Mass including Black Mass
Many ghosts are described as 'foggy', 'misty' or 'indistinct' in their appearance. Some appear this way because they are only partially materialized, but in this case the ghosts are fully manifest. Black or grey masses are often seen at haunted locations and can be photographed.

Gremlin
First reported during the Second World War (1939–45) by airmen on dangerous flying missions, gremlins appeared aboard aircraft as misty figures. It is generally accepted that they are benign spirits, as they do little other than play the odd prank. More recently, sightings have been reported in large factories – perhaps this is where the term 'A gremlin in the works' originates?

Below: *Unique to Dartmoor, the Hairy Hands are an alarming haunting that have been blamed for many road accidents on the B3212.*

Above: *The Scottish kelpie appears mostly in the form of a beautiful horse that drowns its prey once its victim is astride.*

Hag of the Dribble
This hideous haunting from Wales is known locally as 'Gwrach-y-rhibyn'. It manifests in the form of an ugly old hag with a hunched back and long claw-like fingers. Her high-pitched voice spells death to anyone who hears her cry. Hags of the Dribble tend to attach themselves to old Welsh families. Among those currently haunted by these family ghosts are the De Clares of Caerphilly Castle near Cardiff and the Stradlings of St Donats Castle in Glamorgan. One well-known haunt of a Hag of the Dribble is the crumbling ruins of Pennard Castle in West Glamorgan.

Haint
Negative energy that coalesces is known as a haint. A haint is found in an environment where extreme torment or negative emotion has been played out.

Hairy Hands
This peculiar and horrific haunting takes place on the B3212 near Two Bridges on Dartmoor. It takes the form of two large disembodied hairy hands which have been blamed for grabbing the handlebars of motorcycles and causing them to crash. Indeed, there have been numerous sightings of hairy hands on this stretch of road over the years. The most famous was in 1924, when a young couple were staying overnight in a caravan by the side of the road. The woman was woken by a scratching noise and when she looked up she saw two hands crawling up the side of the caravan window! The woman rapidly made the sign of the holy cross and the fiendish phantom dissipated.

Jack-in-Irons
This famous English ghost has been sighted in the quiet roads of Yorkshire. Jack-in-Irons is a tall, demonic-looking ghost swathed in chains, a rarity in ghostlore despite common misconception. These frightening phantoms delight in jumping out on travellers who are foolish enough to be out alone at night.

Jimmy Squarefoot
This spectre is unique to the Isle of Man, where it used to manifest as a large phantom pig on which a cruel giant would ride. More contemporary sightings describe him as a human figure with a pig's head with large tusks. The spirit is known to be completely harmless.

Kelpie
Kelpie is the name given to spectral water hauntings that take the form of horses in order to lure their prey onto their backs. When their passenger is on board, they plunge beneath the water to drown their rider. Legend has it that if you can put a bridle on a kelpie you may command it as your helper, but if it subsequently escapes it will curse its former master and escape back to the river world. Kelpies derive from Scottish folklore, and also have the ability to manifest as wild-looking men.

La Milloraine
This huge, white phantom was known to haunt the

Touraine region of France, although its appearance was never ascertained. It was believed to be feminine and brought with it grievous trouble for anyone who glimpsed it. It is also referred to as 'Demoiselle' in some accounts.

Lham-Dearg (Ghost of the Bloody Hand)

The Ghost of the Bloody Hand is a frightening phantasm that haunts the Glenmore region of Scotland. It is sometimes called Lyerg, and is known to take the form of a male figure in the uniform of a soldier. It has a bloody red hand and challenges all who see it to a fight. It is alleged to have killed three brothers in 1669.

Lorelei

Germany's most famous spectre is a beguiling and beautiful female ghost who appears atop a rock above the River Rhine in Hesse-Nassau. The spectre sings a melody so enchanting that it causes sailors to lose all sense of direction and crash their vessels on the rocks beneath her.

Mara

These evil spirits are recorded in the ghostlore of northern and western France. They are alleged to torment people during the night by taking on a misty form and settling on top of them bringing terrible nightmares. Other accounts tell of these spooks manifesting as naked women to give their male prey erotic dreams!

Mura-Mura

These ancestral spirits of Australia watch over the weather and must be treated with respect lest they prevent rain from falling on dry crops.

Night Man

This friendly ghost is native to the Isle of Man. It forewarns of storms by manifesting as a misty shape or by crying out.

Nixie

These water ghosts are native to Germany, where they haunt large stretches of water and appear as any shape they choose, but often with a human body and the tail of a fish. Providing they are presented with a yearly sacrifice they will stay well away from humankind.

Below: *Reported in all areas of Britain, phantom hounds have many names, but sightings generally have one meaning– an ill omen.*

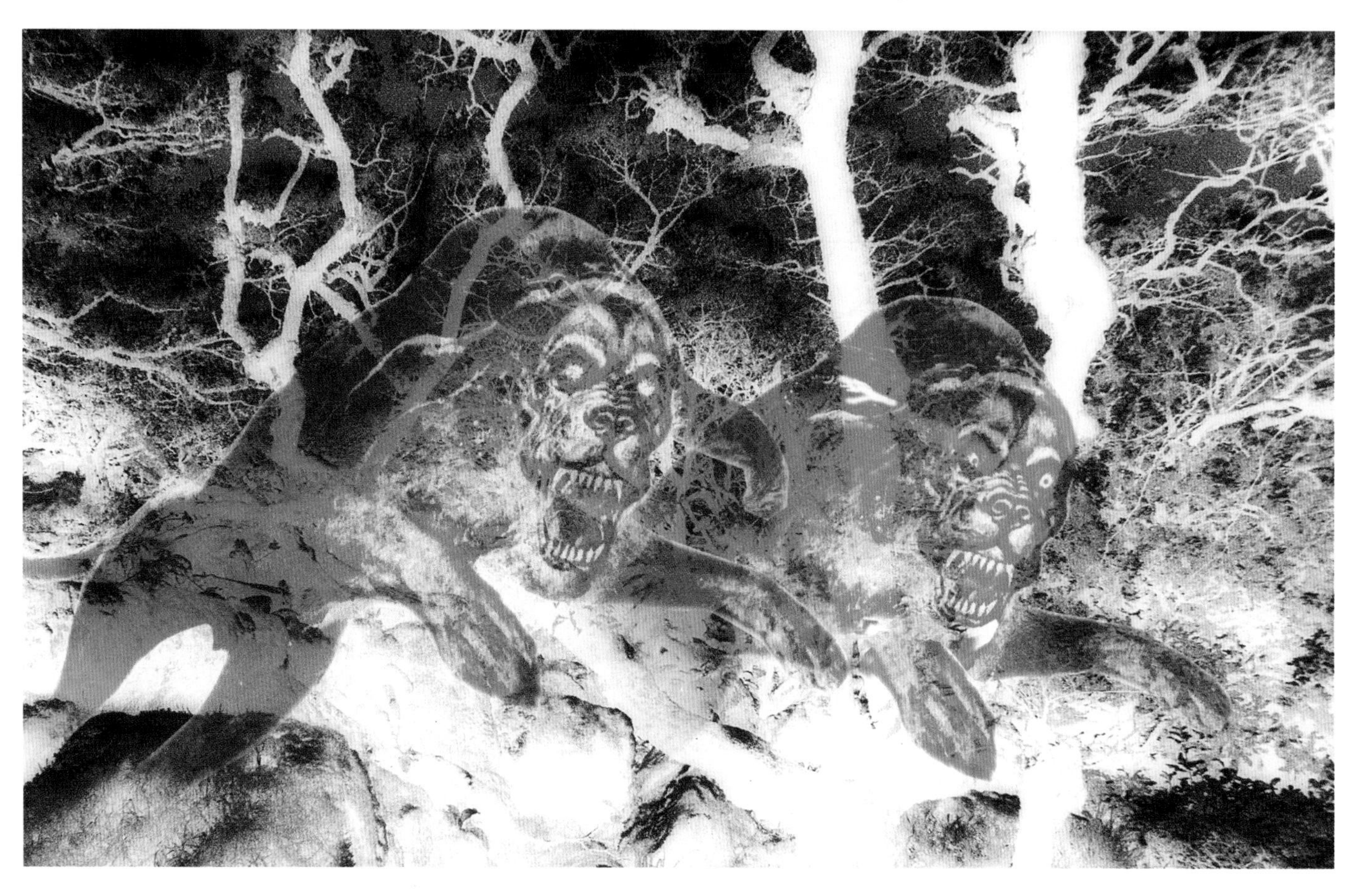

Above: *Ireland is haunted by shape-shifting ghosts known as pookhas. They have been known to appear in a multitude of forms, varying from horses and goats to eagles and bats (see page 50).*

Nuggle
As with the kelpie, nuggles appear in the form of a horse but, unlike kelpies, their aim is not to drown mortals but merely to play with them in the waters before disappearing in a flash of blue light. They are native to the Shetland Isles.

Old Hag
Records of this kind of haunting stretch way back in time and are often confused with sleep paralysis. Legend has it that these hags creep into windows at night and attack sleepers, waking them up and temporarily paralyzing them.

Old Scarf
This Norfolk haunting makes a nuisance of itself by annoyingly prodding and pushing its victims. It is an invisible presence that roams the coastal areas and was recently held responsible for turning a family out of their caravan in Great Yarmouth!

Phantom Bell Ringer
Several English families are haunted by a phantom bell ringer. The Pine-Coffin family of Portledge in Devon is one such family where the spirit either rings the bells in the family home or the local church to signal that a family death is approaching.

Phantom Hound or Black Dog
Commonly accepted as an omen of death, Black Dogs have been seen all over Britain where they have been given many different names. In Norfolk they are called Black Shuck, Snarleyyow and Galley Trot. Cornish folk know them as Dandy Dogs. In Sheffield they are called Gabriel Hounds. The Welsh know them as Cwn and Ci Annwn. On Dartmoor, many sightings are reported and here they are Wisht Hounds or Yeth Hounds. Yorkshire has named Black Dog ghosts Barguest, but in other northern counties they are called Padfoot, Cappel, Gytrash or Skriker. The strangest term for these unusual ghosts is Sky Yelper and Moddey Dhoo, the latter being the name given to the Black Dog that haunts Peel Castle on the Isle Of Man.

Above: *The appearance of St Elmo's Fire signifies that the worst of a storm is over, that is unless it attached itself to a sailor, which is an indication that the sailor's life will be cut short.*

Actor **William Shatner** had a close encounter with a ghost while out riding a motorbike in the desert with some friends. William was joined by a lone rider just before he struck a rock and crashed, badly injuring himself and his bike. His friends were too far ahead of him to notice his plight but strangely, after a short while, his pain diminished and he was able to walk his bike and himself to a petrol station. He asked them to fix his bike but they said there was nothing wrong with it! Upon inspection it was in perfect working order. William caught up with his friends and asked them where the lone rider had gone, but to his amazement they had not seen him. Later that day he saw the ghost on the horizon waving a final goodbye...

In Europe these phantasms are known as Hell Hounds and the sound of their howling is a sign of death to those who hear it. In Africa they are known as Wolhaarhond and, once again, they are an ill omen to those who see them.

Pookha

A pookha is a famous Irish ghost that can shape-shift its manifestation to any form; from horse to goat, from donkey to bull and from eagle to bat. These spirits haunt old ruins and isolated rural areas. Many places in Ireland are known as 'poula phouka' or 'hole of the pookha'. A famous site of a pookha haunting is a waterfall in County Wicklow. Information varies from area to area as to the behaviour of these ghosts, but it is generally agreed that they range from being mischievous or dangerous.

Quinn's Light

A strange glowing light the size of a bird that flies in circles before disappearing. It haunts many areas of the Australian bush, but its purpose is unknown.

St Elmo's Fire

Similar to Will-o'-the-Wisp (see page 52) in appearance, this phenomenon is a sea-borne haunting that appears in the masts of sailing ships as an eerie blue light. Its manifestation signifies that the worst of a storm is over. It is believed to be sent by St Elmo – the patron saint of Mediterranean sailors – hence its name. If the 'fire' moves down the mast and attaches itself to a sailor it is a sign that the sailor's life will be short-lived.

Shin

Shins are Chinese ghosts that are said to be tormenting and evil. In China, people leave offerings outside their homes in the hope that the shins will take the bribe and move on. They are said to have no chins!

Shock

In Suffolk, there are records of this English ghost, which looks like a small dog or donkey with a mane and large eyes. There were several recorded sightings of these ghosts at the turn of the 20th century.

Shojo

These Japanese sea ghosts haunt the oceans, making merry with their favourite drink, sake. It is said that theses ghosts have vivid red hair and that you can lure them with a bottle of sake. They are alleged to spend their existence dancing among the waves and drinking to their spectral hearts' content.

Smoke Ghosts

Smoke Ghosts are well known and recorded in the annals of psychic research. A famous smoke ghost has been witnessed at the Tower of London. They can either manifest as the smell of smoke, often because the person dies by burning to death, or appearing as a cloud of smoke which moves in a way dissimilar to natural smoke.

Tanwedd

This strange Welsh phantom manifests as an eerie ball of phosphorescent light that hovers over the homes of those who are about to experience severe misfortune. If the tanwedd descends onto the building itself it is taken as a sure sign that one or more of the inhabitants is about to die.

Tokolosh

A South African spirit of the waters, the tokolosh appears in the form of a hairy black shape that moves silently and shuns sunlight. Its temperament is cruel and it has the ability to become invisible at will.

Tolaeth

This Welsh haunting is only heard, although the sound varies from one report to another. Sometimes a tolaeth will create the phenomenon of footfall, at other times it makes a dragging, knocking or rapping sound. In all accounts the noisy ghost makes its way to the door of a room where someone is about to pass over to the other side.

Umi Bozu

This phantasm is a giant sea ghost of Japanese origin. It appears as a hideous giant figure with a shaved head and bulbous eyes. Its name means 'priest' or 'monk'.

Virika

A Native American Indian elemental spirit that has a small red-coloured body and enormous vampire-like teeth. Also called Bauta in some accounts, they roam around making a gibbering noise. Virikas have been compared to fictional vampires, as they are reported to have a liking for human blood. Belief in this is so deep in many places that people leave offerings of fresh

Below: *The strange manifestation of dancing lights is known in folklore as Will-o'-the-Wisp, and it is reputed to bring death to those foolish enough to follow it (see page 52).*

meat to prevent the virikas from attacking men.

A famous case of this type of ghost comes from Romania (as with all ghosts, virikas can travel), where a girl named Eleonore Zugun was plagued by a virika for several years, regularly sustaining bite wounds from it.

Water Wraith

Native to Scotland, these appear in the form of ugly old women dressed in green who scowl at anyone who dares to look upon them.

Wendigo

In Canada these ghosts are feared, for they devour human flesh, especially that of young children. They haunt the woods and forests and are of malicious intent.

Will-o'-the-wisp

Also known as Foolish Fire – *Ignis Fatuus* – and Jack-o'-Lantern, appearances of this widespread phenomena are recorded throughout European ghostlore and beyond. In Australia the phenomena is known as Min-Min Lights.

The spirit manifests as dancing lights and is most often witnessed in marshes or graveyards. Will-o'-the-Wisp is believed to bring about death if followed, and legend has it that it is the ghost of Will the Smith, a man so evil that he was refused entry to both Heaven and Hell upon his death. He is now condemned to walk the earth for eternity with only a flickering light to guide his path.

Yellow Man

A French ghost that appears as a yellow glowing figure with red marks upon its throat. Recorded sightings of these ghosts go back to 1870 when one appeared shortly before the outbreak of the Franco-Prussian War. Another was seen prior to the assassination of President Carnot in 1894. Their appearance warns that their native France is under threat in some way.

Phenomena Caused by Elemental Ghosts

- Animal Phenomena
- Befriending Phenomena
- Camera Phenomena
- Disembodied Voices
- Displacement of Objects
- Door Phenomena
- Electromagnetic Variations
- Following Phenomena
- Footfall
- Ghostprints
- Intelligent or Random Knocking, Banging, Scratching or Rapping
- Intense Unpleasant Atmosphere
- Psychic Breezes or Wind
- Psychic Echo
- Screams, Cries, Moans or Wails
- Spectral Scents
- Sound Mimicking
- Tactual Phenomena
- Temperature Variations
- Temporary Witness Paralysis

MISCELLANEOUS GHOST PHENOMENA

Curse

Curses are an integral part of Englsih ghost lore, and they are many and varied. Curses are created by extreme intent being focused on one person or family during a period of emotional turmoil.

One such curse affected the Talbot family of Alton Towers. At a grand ball in the Banqueting Hall, the 15th Earl of Shrewsbury hosted nobility and royalty. Into their midst came an old man, hoping to earn a night's keep by telling their fortunes. But he was mocked and rejected by the company, so he turned to the host and said, 'Every time a branch falls from the giant oak by your entrance, so will a member of your family fall and die.' The next day, the superstitious earl had all the tree's branches chained. Legend has it that, despite this, when branches fell, members of the family died.

Other tales tell of inanimate objects being cursed.

Ghost Hole

In my research, this amazing phenomenon is unique. A witness of a ghost hole told me that she was looking out of a bedroom window in a house known to be haunted and when she turned back to leave the room half the floor had disappeared and in its place was a gaping chasm. After a few seconds the ghost hole disappeared and the floor returned to normal!

Indelible Bloodstain

Reports of these peculiar ghostly occurrences span the British Isles. Indelible bloodstains are caused by some evil deed and can never be removed. In many instances, new wood has been laid to eradicate a supernatural

Above *The red stain on the tomb of believed witch Dame Ann Smith in St Michael's Church, Edmonthorpe, Leicestershire is said to represent a cut she received when she turned herself into a cat.*

stain but in each case the stain has reappeared on the floorboards.

One example of this phenomena is at a house called Berain in Llanefydd in Denbighshire. In the 16th century it was the home of one Catrin Tudur who had seven husbands – all of whom she is said to have murdered in order to increase her personal wealth. She dispatched her spouses in a novel and particularly unpleasant manner – by pouring molten lead into their ears as they slept. One of the husbands woke just as Catrin was about do the deed, so she was forced to improvize – with a large knife! Ever since there has been an indelible bloodstain on the oak panelling that can never be washed away.

Phenomena Caused by Miscellaneous Ghost Phenomena

- Animal Phenomena
- Camera Phenomena
- Following Phenomena
- Ghostprints
- Intense Unpleasant Atmosphere
- Physical Displacement of the World as We Perceive It
- Psychic Breezes or Wind
- Psychic Echo
- Screams, Cries, Moans or Wails
- Temperature Variations

To Catch a Ghost

THE ESSENTIAL GHOST HUNTER'S KIT

CANDLES

Candles are essential but dangerous, therefore extreme care should be taken when using them. Candles can be used to detect paranormal breezes – the flame will show you in which direction a breeze is blowing – and to light areas of investigation as an electrical light source is not usually appropriate. Using candles in this way can identify psychic breezes that come from nowhere, and can also indicate where there are natural breezes at the beginning of an investigation.

Candles

CHALK

Chalk is used to mark the position of large items of furniture by making a light line round the objects in question. Although rare, furniture has been reported to move during investigations.

COMPASS

A compass has a variety of uses: it can help determine the exact position of the location of your investigation, it can be used for mapping and for detecting areas of magnetic fluctuation. However, for the latter an EMF meter (see page 59) is a much better tool for the task.

DOWSING RODS AND PENDULUMS

These are a useful, fun addition to any ghost hunter's kit. Dowsing is an ancient form of locating things using the geopathic stress – the natural radiation that rises up through the earth and is distorted by weak electromagnetic fields created by subterranean running water, certain mineral concentrations, fault lines and underground cavities of the land itself. In the past, dowsers were used to locate water and oil and, even in today's modern world of industry, dowsers are still used when mechanical devices fail. There are two primary ways of dowsing: using a pair of dowsing rods or using a dowsing pendulum.

Dowsing rods

Dowsing rods are long and straight in shape and are usually made of thick wire. The dowser holds a rod in each hand and trains them to his or her vibration by concentrating on influencing the rods to cross over each other – to indicate a 'Yes' answer – and then concentrating on influencing them to part – to indicate a 'No' answer.

Once the rods are trained to the vibration of the dowser, he or she walks around an area holding the rods out horizontally while concentrating on the task in question. The rods can be used to locate ley lines and psychic epicentres – the spots where psychic energy is strongest and, therefore, the possible location of a paranormal entity. The rods will cross over each other when something is located. As well as mapping ley lines, it is also possible to pinpoint underground streams, as these may be the cause of natural effects, such as cold spots, that might otherwise be wrongly attributed to paranormal activity.

Dowsing pendulum

Dowsing pendulums are used in a different way to dowsing rods. The pendulum must be held completely still in one hand so that it does not sway or move in any direction. The dowser then concentrates on telling the pendulum to spin in a circular movement to indicate a 'Yes' answer. Then the dowser tells the pendulum to stop, at which point it should stop almost instantly. The dowser then asks the pendulum to sway from left to right – this being a 'No' answer. Once the dowser has trained the pendulum, it can be used to answer questions about a location's history or hauntings.

Another use of the dowsing pendulum is to walk around a location while simultaneously asking the pendulum to spin when it crosses a ley line or psychic epicentre. Some mediums use a pendulum to dowse answers and others to dowse locations. Either way is useful and can add a great sense of fun to a ghost hunt.

FLOUR AND DUSTING BRUSH

This simple experiment is most effective if set up in the right place. Flour is lightly brushed onto surfaces and floors in the vicinity of a ghost's activity, the area is then left for a period before being returned to to check if the flour has been disturbed.

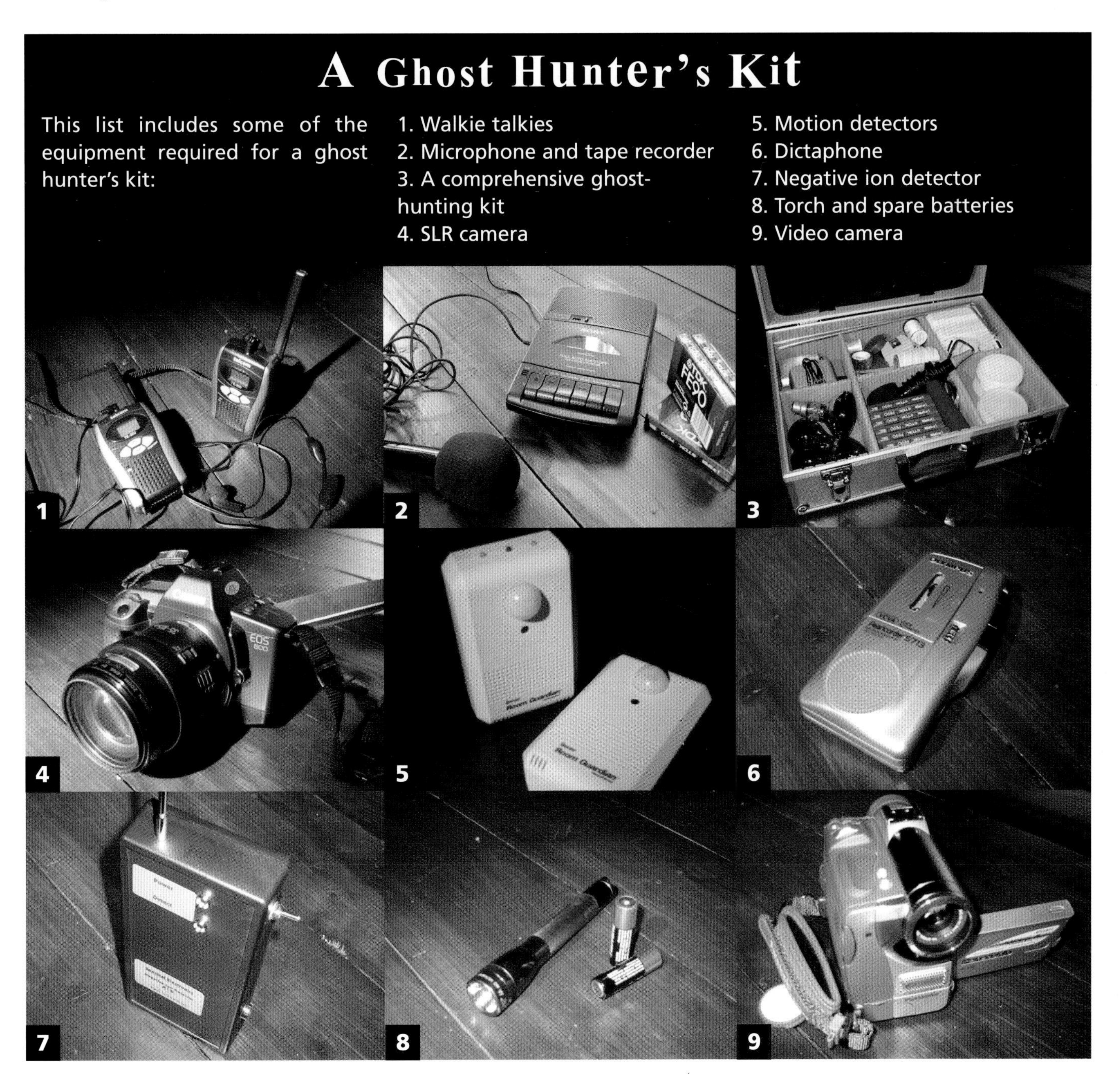

A Ghost Hunter's Kit

This list includes some of the equipment required for a ghost hunter's kit:

1. Walkie talkies
2. Microphone and tape recorder
3. A comprehensive ghost-hunting kit
4. SLR camera
5. Motion detectors
6. Dictaphone
7. Negative ion detector
8. Torch and spare batteries
9. Video camera

Compass

Flour dusting

GRAPH PAPER

This is essential for mapping the entire area under investigation.

OUIJA BOARDS

Ouija boards are an ancient means of communication between the world of the living and the world of the dead. They became popular as a parlour game during the heyday of Victorian spiritualism, and have since been manufactured and sold as a board game.

There are several versions available today, but the best is the original design, which is now produced by the board-game company Hasbro in the United States. The word 'ouija' comes from the French word *Oui* and the German word *Ja*, both of which mean 'Yes'. The board can be used to get 'Yes' or 'No' responses to direct questions. Alternatively, answers are sometimes spelled out using the letters marked on the board.

Ouija boards are sometimes used with a planchette, which is a board mounted on two casters on which each sitter taking part lightly places a finger. Occasionally, an upturned glass is used in place of the planchette. There is no doubt that ouija boards work, but how they work and where the information comes from is another matter.

Where does the information come from?

The truth is we don't actually know the answer to this question. Mediums, psychics and spiritualists will tell you the information is being imparted through the board from a spirit on the other side. While this may be the case, it is important to remember that it is just as likely that someone is pushing the planchette or glass intentionally. It is also possible that the sitters are communicating telepathically and are unconsciously answering each others' 'secret' questions by manipulating the planchette without realizing they are doing so.

Are ouija boards dangerous?

We have all heard disturbing stories involving ouija boards, but when it comes down to facts it is usually 'a friend of a friend' that was involved and not the person relating the story themselves. The stories about

The Ouija Board Test

Here is a simple test I designed years ago in order to check whether the information coming through a ouija board is indeed from the beyond, or from the minds of the sitters.

1. Take a book that no one participating has ever read or looked at.
2. Open the book randomly, face-down so that no one can see the page that has been opened.
3. Place the book face-down on the floor.
4. Ask the ouija board to spell out the first ten words from the top of the left-hand page of the book in the correct order.

In my experience this has never worked and I have tried it hundreds of times. This does not mean the ouija board is not communicating with a spirit, however. What it does mean is that the information given can be incorrect and, therefore, should not be trusted or taken literally.

Ouija board

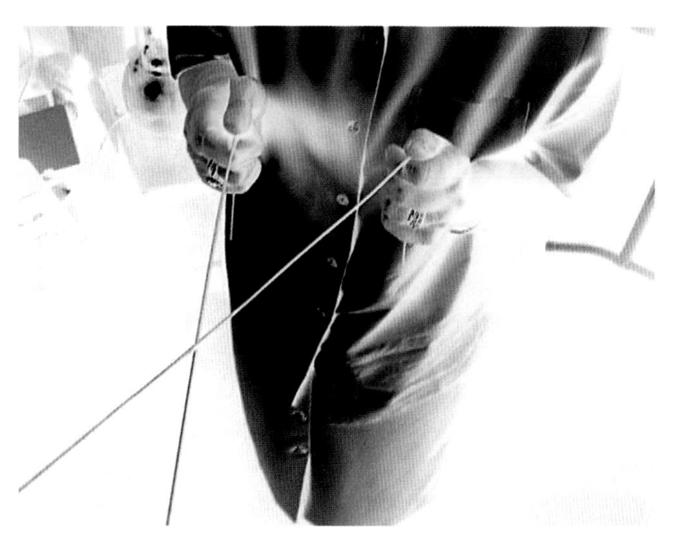

Dowsing rods

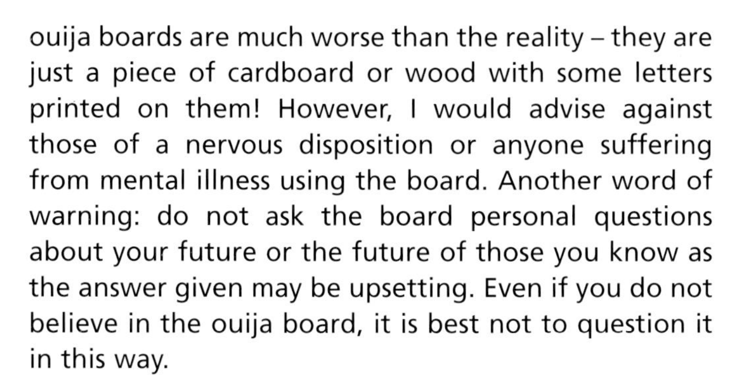

ouija boards are much worse than the reality – they are just a piece of cardboard or wood with some letters printed on them! However, I would advise against those of a nervous disposition or anyone suffering from mental illness using the board. Another word of warning: do not ask the board personal questions about your future or the future of those you know as the answer given may be upsetting. Even if you do not believe in the ouija board, it is best not to question it in this way.

Making your own ouija board

Many investigators and researchers make their own ouija boards by placing cards in a circle on a table. The letters of the alphabet and the words 'Yes' and 'No' are written on the cards. I have used this technique many times and it works just as well as having a traditional board. Remember to put the cards on a flat surface so that the glass or planchette can move around freely.

PENS, PENCILS AND NOTEBOOK

Never go on a ghost hunt without the means to record everything that happens in explicit detail. You can never have enough notebooks, pens and pencils. Make sure everyone on the hunt has his or her own pens and notebooks so everyone can record what they see and experience. Use a diary format with dates and times logged for each event.

ROOM THERMOMETERS

Temperature variations often occur in the presence of a ghost and, although we can naturally sense that the temperature has changed, in order to record this accurately a room thermometer is needed. To get a truly precise reading it is useful to use two or three thermometers in different areas of the study site. Once you have decided where to put them it is simply a question of checking them regularly for variations. Of course, you need to keep one with you, too, in case you notice a sudden temperature change.

It is normal for the temperature to fluctuate by a few degrees and for the temperature to drop gradually throughout a night-time investigation. What you are looking for are extreme variations in a short space of time. Normal mercury-based thermometers are good enough for this.

SLR CAMERA

An SLR (single lens reflex) camera is probably the most important piece of equipment in a ghost hunter's kit. It can be used to photograph the layout of an area, the rooms, the objects and the people taking part in the investigation; it can also be used to photograph ghosts themselves. SLR cameras have film and, therefore, negatives, which can be tampered with, so it is worth bearing this in mind when presenting evidence to critics. SLR cameras are preferable to digital cameras, however, as they are not prone to malfunction in a place that suffers from the jinx factor.

STRING, COTTON, FISHING WIRE AND STICKY TAPE

These have a variety of uses, but are particularly handy for securing windows and doors. To secure an area, use sticky tape to fix a piece of fishing wire across a closed door. If, when you return, the wire has been broken, you will know that the area has been visited by someone or something. Black or white cotton can also be used to secure areas by attaching it loosely across archways and passageways; if anything solid passes through them it will break or dislodge the cotton.

This is a good way of catching out anyone who is trying to trick you, as well as helping you to identify where solid apparitions have passed.

SUGAR

Sugar is used during ghost hunts to reveal ghoststeps. Place a single layer of sugar on the ground in an area where ghosts are known to walk. Put a sheet of paper over the sugar so that when something solid walks over it the sugar will crunch. Of course, this will only work if the ghost is solid.

TAPE MEASURE

A tape measure is used to record accurately the size of doorways, windows and other features when mapping the area. It can also be used to measure items such as haunted objects, apports or asports.

TAPE RECORDER

A tape recorder is useful for recording long séance or ouija board sessions. The tape can be played back at a later date, and the contents can be analyzed and transcribed onto paper or a computer. They can also be left recording for long periods of time in empty rooms. When the tapes are played back, there may be sounds that cannot be explained. Tape recorders can also be used to capture EVPs, but a dictaphone (see below) is better for this.

Using a trigger object

TORCH

A torch will help you to move safely around dark locations, such as the haunted hallways of a medieval castle or a Victorian manor house.

TRIGGER OBJECTS

It is always necessary to set up trigger objects during a ghost hunt. Try to use something relevant to the haunting. For example, if the ghost is that of a monk, try using a crucifix. Other effective trigger objects include pieces of material, flowers and coins familiar to the believed spectre.

You need to place trigger objects where they will not be disturbed by other investigators. Ideally this should be in a secured area, but this is not always possible. Once you have decided where to place your object, place it on a plain piece of paper and draw round it so that you can see its exact position. Leave the object unattended for some time; on your return check to see if it has been moved or, indeed, if it has been asported. This experiment is particularly effective in ghost research and it has brought spectacular results on many occasions.

WATCH

All investigators should wear a reliable watch, and these should be synchronized at the beginning of an investigation with other members of the investigating team so that the time of any logged sightings or experiences can be cross-checked against everyone else's movements at the time of the sighting or experience.

THE ADVANCED GHOST HUNTER'S KIT

For the more experienced and dedicated ghost hunter there are a number of other gadgets and devices that can be utilized during ghost investigations.

DICTAPHONE

A dictaphone is a great way of recording interviews with witnesses. It saves time in writing everything down on a notepad. They are also very useful for recording séances (see page 61) and EVP sessions.

Electronic Voice Phenomena

Electronic Voice Phenomena (EVPs) is the term used to define voice recordings that have been recorded at ELF (Extremely Low Frequency), a frequency that the human ear cannot hear and that the human voice cannot create. In order to record EVPs, walk around the location asking questions of the ghost(s), pausing after each question to allow time for an unheard response and recording potential answers on a dictaphone or

EVP Range

Human voice	300–3,000 Hertz
Extremely Low Frequency (ELF)	1–300 Hertz

portable tape recorder. On playing the recording back, it is often possible to hear noises or voices responding to the posed questions that could not be heard at the time. Many researchers believe these voices to be those of the dead.

During an investigation at Netley Abbey in Hampshire in early 2003 I had a startling experience while attempting to record EVPs. A ghost answered my questions in a gruff loud booming voice, it sounded unpleasant and aggravated so we decided to leave soon after it was recorded. At another study of a haunted inn in Gloucestershire, I managed to record knockings in response to a series of questions. The knocks were not heard at the time, but on playing back the tape they were getting more and more impatient each time we asked for a response.

Anything heard on the recording when played back at normal recorded speed but not experienced at the time of recording may be an EVP and should be investigated thoroughly to determine any meaning or message it contains.

A non-EVP occurs when the speed of playback is changed, stretched and shortened to create a voice. They often sound peculiar and require quite a lot of wishful thinking to interpret them as voices. Personally, I do not believe these are anything other than over-enthusiastic researchers finding what they want to find. The best equipment is digital as it does not need tapes and is harder to manipulate fraudulently.

DIGITAL THERMOMETERS

These are the best way of monitoring the ambient temperatures in any environment. They give a clear digital display of the exact temperature and therefore eradicate human error in reading mercury-based thermometers.

Many digital thermometers also have a feature whereby they can record the minimum and maximum temperatures in a room over a given period of time. This is particularly useful if you have several areas under investigation, as it means you do not need to constantly watch the thermometer to record the changes.

EMF METERS

It is generally accepted that ghosts either generate high electromagnetic fields or that they cause electromagnetic energy to fluctuate. As electrical devices also generate electromagnetic fields, high EMFs in the vicinity of an electrical device do not indicate anything unusual. By using an EMF meter it is possible to measure levels of electromagnetic energy in milligauss (the measurement of electromagnetic frequency) on location during a ghost investigation.

Anything over 10 milligauss is considered high and potentially harmful, but it may also indicate a paranormal presence.

EMF meters are notorious for giving false readings and, therefore, it is best to spend as much money as you can afford in order to get a reliable product.

Digital thermometer

EMF Meter Range

Typical house	0.1–0.3 milligauss
Possible ghost presence	2.0+ milligauss

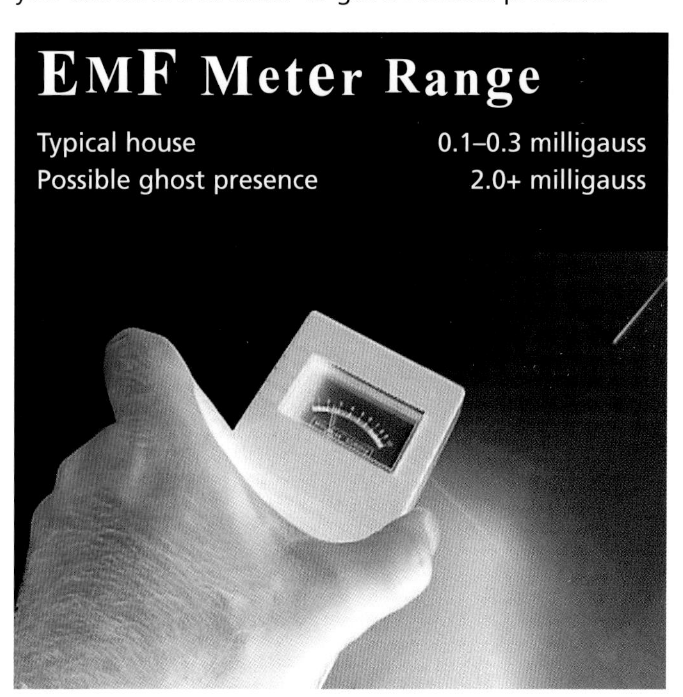

Above: *A live observation unit, such as this one used by the Ghost Research Foundation International, can be a valuable addition to a ghost-hunting team.*

GEOPHYSICAL EQUIPMENT

This is not usually available to the amateur ghost hunter, but when used it can produce remarkable results. I have been fortunate enough to work with a geophysics team on several investigations where they have detected anomalous movements in areas under observation that could not have been caused by humans, animals or air displacement – in other words, something large and invisible! Geophysical equipment can also identify where buildings used to be and can detect any hidden cavities beneath the ground that may house buried objects or human remains.

ION DETECTOR

These devices can be adjusted to measure positive and negative ions. Similar to EMF meters, the ion detector will measure a high disturbance of ions in the air when spirit energy is present. These devices are great for investigations because they are sensitive to naturally occurring elements, such as radiation, electrical storms and radon.

Ion detectors are used to check whether anomalies caught on camera actually have any physical density to them. After taking a base reading of the natural ion count in the area, regular readings must be taken at timed slots which can later be compared with any timed filming or photography of an anomaly. These readings can then be compared to the earlier base reading to see if the ion count changed, thus providing evidence that the anomaly has density even though it is not visible to the human eye.

LAPTOP COMPUTER

A laptop computer can be used to instantly log activity as it is witnessed or can be connected to a video or other sensing devices to record changes in the atmosphere, such as movement and temperature variations. A computer is also useful for creating charts, graphs and reports of your findings.

LIVE OBSERVATION UNIT

This is essentially a Closed Circuit Television system that can be set up to observe an area while it is displayed on a monitor elsewhere. This is particularly useful as there is evidence that human interaction with a room or area can lessen ghost activity. By using a live observation unit, you can leave the room or area to settle but still maintain a watch over it. Some systems also include remote-control cameras so that camera angles can be manipulated.

MEDIUMS AND PSYCHICS

As in any field, there are good and bad mediums and psychics. At their best, mediums can provide excellent evidence of the survival of the spirit beyond death and give much comfort to grieving relatives and widowed partners. Bad mediums can frighten, intimidate and manipulate the vulnerable, and charge large sums of money for doing so. There are also many mediums and psychics who mean no harm but who simply are not the genuine article. Please note that true mediums rarely need to advertise.

Reputable mediums can add greater depth to a study and can often steer the researcher in a completely new direction. They are particularly useful on location when they can tune into a site's ghosts by walking around the various rooms and other areas sensing the entities and verbalizing their psychic feelings. These 'walk-arounds' should be recorded either on a dictaphone or tape recorder or, even better, on a video camera. During investigations by the Ghost Research Foundation International (GRFI) this picture is transmitted to a monitor in the base room so that the whole investigation team can see what the medium is picking up as it happens. After all, it simply is not practical to have 30 people following a medium on his or her walk-around!

MOVEMENT SENSORS

These can be bought relatively cheaply and can be used for three purposes: to catch out anyone acting fraudulently; to sense the movement of objects caused by ghosts; and to catch the movement of ghosts themselves. Movement sensors work like common intruder alarms: when something disturbs the area covered by the sensor an alarm is set off.

NEGATIVE ION GENERATOR

Negative ion generators are used to artificially create an atmosphere that is conducive to a manifestation. One of the distinct differences between fresh outdoor air and stale indoor air is the balance of negative and positive ions.

The freshest outdoor air has high concentrations of negative ions (oxygen molecules with an extra electron attached) and relatively few positive ions (oxygen with

Laptop computer

an electron stripped away). High concentrations of negative ions are found in evergreen forests, around waterfalls, and in the air after a thunderstorm. At the other extreme, positive ions are found in high concentrations inside closed, air-conditioned and heated buildings, and outdoors in cities during the rush hour (as pollution depletes negative ions).

Ghostly experiences and sightings are often reported during thunderstorms – when there are lots of negative ions in the atmosphere – so there may be a link between high negative ions in the atmosphere and ghostly activity taking place, which is why this piece of equipment is included in an advanced investigator's kit.

0-LUX OR INFRA-RED VIDEO CAMERA

These have become increasingly popular in the paranormal community over the last few years, especially as they have recently become significantly cheaper. They can be set up to monitor visual activity in low-light or even zero-light conditions. Footage of many stages of ghost manifestation have been caught on video using this equipment.

Always make sure you have plenty of fresh tapes. Using the same tape more than once will leave you open to criticism from sceptics as images from one recording may be visible in another. Digital equipment is the best for this kind of observation as it is less likely to be affected by problems such as image doubling. However, digital equipment can be 'jinxed'.

SÉANCES

Séances are usually managed by experienced mediums or psychics, who are used to attuning themselves to the

Above: *Séances were popular during the spiritualists' heyday – the turn of the 20th century – but they can still be useful for contacting the spirit world today.*

higher spiritual vibrations needed for a successful séance session. Anyone can hold a séance, but its usefulness will be directly related to the experience of those in charge.

Usually held in semi- or complete darkness, séances originated from the spiritualist movement, which was at its height at the turn of the 20th century. The person in charge of the séance will call forth spirits from the other side and they will communicate with the sitters through either movement of objects, tactual phenomena, sounds or manifestations.

In truth, good séances are as rare as good mediums. The sitters sit in a circle holding hands and attempt to pool their bio-electric energy using thought. Basically, this means visualizing an imagined energy rushing round the circle through the bodies of the sitters. Many believe that ghosts can use this energy to create phenomena and it acts like a battery of power that attracts them to the room.

Using the collective energy of the sitters also means that individual sitters will not feel drained after the experience, as is often the case when people have encounters with ghosts when they are alone. Various things may occur during a séance, including the temporal voluntary possession of the medium when the ghost will talk directly to the sitters through the mouth of the medium – this is called physical mediumship.

In extreme circumstances, there have been reports of the body shape and face of the medium altering during a séance of particular power. Information learned through séance situations should be verified with historical research and not taken as fact. Ghost hunters should also be aware of potential fraud in séance situations.

WALKIE-TALKIES

These are invaluable for keeping in contact with other members of a ghost hunt and to let everyone know exactly what is being experienced.

SETTING UP AN INVESTIGATION

After your preliminary research in local libraries and archives to collate as much data on the given site as possible, it is usual to carry out at least one night-time investigation. These are sometimes called vigils and normally go on all night. If a case warrants it, then several vigils should be conducted, preferably with the same team of people, in order to be be able to compare and contrast.

Once on site, firstly set up a base room where the team can relax and where all the equipment can be stored. This will also be where the live observation unit will be set up, if you have one. Once a base has been established it is a good idea for everyone to familiarize themselves with the location and its layout, and someone should begin mapping the area before photographs are taken. Interviews with any witnesses normally follow and then the actual investigation commences. An investigation consists of several teams spending short periods of time in designated areas and recording their findings, observations and experiences in minute detail. It's a good idea to take baseline readings of the naturally occurring electromagnetic energies and temperatures around the site.

SENIOR INVESTIGATORS

All Ghost Research Foundation International (GRFI) investigations are presided over by a senior investigator, who is usually the president, vice president or secretary or their designate. It is the responsibility of the senior investigator to maintain the reputation of the GRFI at any given location and to ensure that all agreed techniques of investigation are carried out correctly. It is also their responsibility to oversee any links with the media and not to let these take precedence over the investigation itself.

The senior investigator will organize participants into small groups (if numbers allow) so that as much of the location can be observed at any one time as possible and also so that everyone can meet the other participants. They will decide where the watch posts and temperature monitoring points will be. The senior investigator will have a walkie talkie, as will each group, so that the entire team can stay in close contact at all times.

At the back of the book there are examples of the standard form used by investigators when interviewing witnesses of paranormal activity.

Participant Instructions For Investigations

It is required that all participants at the GRFI follow some basic outlines for each investigation (unless requested not to do so by the senior investigator):

❶ Participants must remain at their posts for each watch segment and not move from these posts without good reason.

❷ Participants will be posted at different watch posts throughout the investigation.

❸ Participants will re-group in the base room or area between each watch period.

❹ Participants will be given time to take refreshments between watch segments.

❺ Participants **MUST** log all movements, noises, sightings, feelings, etc. in their logbook, including sounds which could have a natural explanation. It is paramount that absolutely everything that occurs is logged, whether it can be explained or not.

❻ Any participant who believes they are observing a paranormal phenomenon should remain still and quiet, taking note of as many details as possible. After doing this, an attempt should be made to communicate with the phenomenon and photograph the area (remember that a lot of anomalous photographs are taken when nothing is actually visible to the human eye at the time). If the phenomenon moves, the participant should attempt to follow it. **DO NOT SHINE A TORCH, MOVE SUDDENLY OR MAKE ANY NOISE** as these seem to dissipate most types of ghost phenomena.

❼ Above all else, never jump to conclusions and remember the first rule of ghost hunting: always look for a natural explanation before looking for a supernatural one.

INVESTIGATION TECHNIQUES

The GRFI has used many different kinds of equipment and testing techniques over the past 12 years, and they have found the following to be the most successful:

AUDIO RECORDING by tape recorder or dictaphone to record inexplicable sounds either heard or not heard at the time, record witness interviews and communications/séances and to capture EVPs.

BREEZE DETECTION carried out with a candle to detect unnatural breeze variations.

CHALK MARKING to detect the anomalous movement of large objects or furniture.

COMMUNICATIONS/SÉANCES to attempt to 'talk' directly to ghosts, normally by the use of a Ouija Board.

DOWSING to detect energy centres, ley lines, etc.

ELECTROMAGNETIC FIELD MONITORING to detect unnatural variations using EMF metres.

FLOUR DUSTING surfaces to catch ghostprints.

FLOUR MARKING objects to detect anomalous movement of small objects.

FRAME OF MIND LOGGING in the participant's logbook with time entries. This is particularly relevant for any sensitive members of the team.

GEOPHYSICAL INVESTIGATION can uncover valuable information, such as previous buildings, hidden rooms and even human remains.

INFRA-RED VIDEO OBSERVATION using digital 0-Lux video camera to film in total darkness.

LOGGING all occurrences in a logbook (or notebook) with time entries for each comment.

MAGNETIC FIELD MONITORING with a compass to detect unnatural variations.

Below: *Candles can be used to monitor breezes of a paranormal nature*

Below: *Detailed maps and plans should always be prepared by one of the ghost-hunting team.*

MAPPING the entire location to show positions of objects, furniture and general floor plans. The map can also be used to indicate watch posts.

MUSICAL ENTICEMENT to encourage ghost phenomena to occur.

PHOTOGRAPHING the entire location before, during and after the investigation.

PSYCHIC/MEDIUM introduced to deepen the spiritual aspect of the investigation; all information should be recorded with attempts to verify it made later.

REMOTE THERMAL SCANNING to detect anomalous unseen presences using a non contact thermometer that measures temperature by firing a laser beam.

SEALING areas where reported phenomena is localized. This is actioned with sticky tape and paper strips signed by the sealer and attached in such a way that any tampering by a human agency would be obvious.

SUGAR TRAP set up to detect anomalous footfall or to catch fraudsters.

TEMPERATURE MONITORING at set points as well as in general areas to detect unnatural variations using thermometers.

TORCHES to illuminate dark locations.

TRIGGER OBJECT PLACEMENT to attract the attention of ghosts.

VIDEO OBSERVATION to catch anomalous images on film and to record witness interviews, general location appearance and communications/séances.

WATCH SYNCHRONIZATION should take place at the start of the investigation to ensure that all time entries in logbooks tally.

WITNESS INTERVIEWS of staff, owners etc. concerning their own experiences or second-hand ones.

Below: *Dusting flour over surfaces can catch ghost-prints, such as this caught at Michelham Priory in 1992.*

Below: *Geophysical equipment can be a useful addition to a serious ghost investigation (see page 60).*

Britain's Most Haunted Places

BRITAIN'S MOST HAUNTED HOUSE

HEOL FANOG, BRECON BEACONS, WALES

The story of the hauntings of Heol Fanog received wide publicity after a full and detailed account of the house, the people who experienced the haunting and the ghosts themselves was published in the excellent book *Testimony* by Mark Chadbourn.

Heol Fanog. The very name strikes fear into the heart of the Rich family who lived there for seven years. There, they were subjected to the terrifying ordeal of living with an evil influence, which almost caused the destruction of their home and their family. Heol Fanog may look like an idyllic Welsh stone farmhouse, but it is not. It is a dark place of fear and phantoms; a place where, according to the Rich family, the forces of pure evil have manifest in every imaginable horrific form.

The Rich family moved from London to the Brecon Beacons in August 1990 and were delighted with their new family home. Bill was an artist and was anticipating a period of renewed inspiration for his work. After a few happy months, things started to change. At first it was the atmosphere in the kitchen, the hub of family life, that was affected. The air would become stale, and the acrid smell of incense mixed with sulphur would engulf the room, which itself would take on a dark and foreboding atmosphere.

Death and the Devil

It was about this time that Bill and his wife, Liz, were told by locals that their new home was believed to be strange. They soon noticed that their electricity bills were unusually and inexplicably high – up to £750 a quarter! – even though the central heating was run on oil and they had an oil-fired Aga for cooking.

Next, their animals mysteriously died: first the pig, then the guinea pig and the goat. Later the cat and dog both went mad.

Other strange incidences started to take place with the number 666 – the number of the Antichrist in the Book of Revelation – cropping up continually. The rent for the house was £699.66, a shopping bill came to £66.66, a car registration read CNT 666 and a lunch cost £6.66. All coincidence perhaps? Or perhaps not.

Over the months, the phenomena increased to the extent that disturbing paranormal events were taking place on a daily basis. These ranged from loud snoring and unexplained sounds to apparitions of

Opposite: *The Rich family suffered seven years of torment, including abnormally high electricity bills, from dark forces at their home in the Brecon Beacons.*

Above: *Horrifying Heol Fanog – the multitude of paranormal activities that have occurred there make it without doubt the most haunted house in Britain.*

strange amorphous black shapes which took numerous forms, including that of a figure – which was seen by Liz and others in the kitchen – and bird of prey shapes.

In desperation, Bill and Liz called in help from everywhere and anywhere. Over several years they were visited by more than 30 experts, including healers, dowsers, psychics and exorcists, all of whom told them that the place was a centre of evil energies that were too powerful to eradicate. Some felt that the site had been used to practise ancient forms of black magic. Others told the family that the kitchen was a portal to the other side and that many of the spirits they were witnessing were coming and going through this gateway and were not directly connected to the house itself. But no-one could stop the hauntings for long.

Finally, psychic Eddie Burks was introduced to them. Eddie is a renowned clairsentient who has investigated many cases of ghosts and hauntings, and it was he who finally made some sense of the horror at Heol Fanog. Before Eddie even visited the site he sensed that several souls were trapped and bound to Heol Fanog and that several dark deeds had been played out there. Through psychic trance Eddie came up with an amazing account of the haunting.

A Bacchanal?

It all began with a stable boy named Thomas Edwards. Thomas was 18 and desperately in love with a maid from Brecon. The two met frequently at night and they would cross the fields to rendezvous. One night the girl did not turn up and Thomas decided to return to his home and place of work at nearby Cwmgwdi Farm. While crossing the fields on that autumn night in 1848 his attention was drawn to a dim light in the trees near the big house known as Heol Fanog Manor; he ventured nearer to see what it was.

While crouching under a bramble bush Thomas's heart began to thump in his chest as he saw a crowd of people drinking red liquid from a chalice and a man dressed in a red cape while a woman lay on top of some kind of altar. He watched awestruck and with mounting fear as he heard them chanting in a strange

Above: *The stones of Heol Fanog Manor were used to build the Rich family's farmhouse, and brought with them a terrifying haunting*

tongue before frantically attacking the woman with knives and bludgeons, brutally killing her and revelling in the mad lunacy of their activity.

He quickly left, running all the way home, and on reaching his straw bed at Cwmgwdi he fell into a troubled sleep. The next day he was woken by his colleague, James Griffiths, to whom he related what he had witnessed. That night, after several ales at the local inn, he let slip the story to others, who gathered round him, eager to hear his account of the satanic rites at Heol Fanog Manor.

Catherine Zeta-Jones once lived in a haunted house in Wales before she was an actress. Each night she would cower under the sheets as unexplained noises echoed around the building. Eventually she persuaded her brother to move in with her to frighten away the ghost!

The Fate of Thomas Edwards

The next morning Thomas was found dead by his master near a dung heap. His corpse was covered in blood and a pitchfork had been thrust mercilessly and repeatedly into his body while an axe blow had been dealt to his head. A confusing trial ensued and finally blame was laid on the shoulders of James Griffiths, who was hung for his murder. It was an unjust trial, for Thomas had actually been silenced by the Satanists for speaking of what he had seen, and James had been the scapegoat.

Decades after the events of Thomas's death, the manor house fell into disrepair. The stone from the house was used to build the smaller farmhouse that the Rich family had moved to. It seems that the evil had been taken from one place to another and that the dark power connected with the manor had now found a new home in the farmhouse.

Eddie believed that the spirits of Thomas, James and countless others were trapped at Heol Fanog in an eternal turmoil from which they could not break free, tormented by the evil manifestations that plagued both the land of the living at the house and the land of the dead in the afterworld. He believed that the cause of the hauntings and other disturbances were the result of murder, satanic worship and evil, which had been played out time after time at Heol Fanog Manor.

After Eddie's visit and subsequent attempt to rescue the trapped spirits, the Rich's searched through local records where they discovered that a local farmhand had been murdered in the mid-1800s by an axe blow to the back of his head.

After seven years of terror, the Rich family finally found the money to leave and fled Heol Fanog for good. They now live a peaceful life 13 miles away. Many have tried to contact the owner of the farmhouse as the publicity surrounding the case aroused great interest in the paranormal community, but apparently he lives far from Heol Fanog on a remote Scottish Island.

BRITAIN'S MOST HAUNTED HALL

LITTLEDEAN HALL, GLOUCESTERSHIRE, ENGLAND

Hidden deep in the ancient Forest of Dean lies Littledean Hall, the oldest and most haunted house in Britain. It dates back to Saxon times, the cellars having once been part of a stronghold that stood on the site. The rest of the hall is an eclectic mix of Norman and medieval architecture, and there is even the remains of a Roman temple – once sacred to the Goddess Sabrina, Protector of the River Severn – in the grounds. Remains of animals have been unearthed here, which psychics say were used in sacrifices as offerings to the goddess.

Below: *Secluded in the Gloucestershire countryside, Littledean Hall is home to several ghosts, the most famous being a small African boy carrying a candle.*

Above: *Ghostly figures have been glimpsed at windows inside haunted Littledean Hall.*

Civil War Spectres

The ghosts at Littledean Hall don't confine themselves to the hall itself, many have been seen in the grounds, including that of a hooded figure that floats across the drive and into the apple orchard. It has been seen in the early hours of the morning and is thought to be the ghost of John Brayne, a Roundhead captain in the English Civil War (1642–9). Brayne is alleged to have disguised himself as a gardener so that he could observe the hall during 1643 when Littledean was used by Prince Maurice as his headquarters for planning the Royalist campaign against the Roundheads. The hall was taken over by Roundhead troops a year later when a massacre, instigated by a panicked soldier, broke out inside the building.

Two of the hall's most famous ghosts exist because of what happened on the day of the massacre, and they have often been seen fighting a ghostly duel in the dining room. One-time owner of the house, Donald Macer-Wright, lived in the house from the age of seven and recalls hearing the sound of clashing swords on a moonlit night. He also remembers the indelible bloodstain on the dining-room floor, which is believed to have been caused by a Civil War skirmish. The wooden floorboards have been replaced and the room carpeted since then, but neither has deterred the ghostly bloodstain which reappeared on the new wood and seeped through the carpet 'like diesel oil'.

Ghosts for Dinner

The dining room is one of the most haunted rooms in the house. It is visited by the ghost of a young child, who cannot be seen only sensed, and another phantom, as yet unidentified, which visited Donald while he was reading in the room one day. He had made a fire using some twigs and wood and had just sat down to read when his dog started to whine and cower in the corner of the room. Then a ghastly smell arose, which Donald described as that of 'putrefying flesh, and very strong'. Then, the fire went out as quickly as if a bucket of water had been thrown on it. By now, the dog was in such distress that Donald let it out of the room and went with it. Ten minutes later he returned to find that the atmosphere had completely lifted, the smell had dissipated and the fire was blazing in its grate. The ghostly presence had gone.

The dining room is also haunted by the spirits of two brothers of the Pyrke family who owned the house from 1664 to 1896. Legend has it they were eating dinner one evening and enjoying a drink when the subject of women came up in conversation. It transpired that they had both become romantically involved with the same girl. As a result they shot each other dead at the table. The family hushed up the affair but the ghosts of the brothers still linger.

A ghost from an earlier period – a monk dressed in a white habit – also frequents the dining room. He is believed to have illegally held the Catholic Mass here during the years of religious intolerance in the 16th century, and his ghost is said to come out of a secret passage and wander from the dining room to the library.

Ladies, Gentlemen and Poltergeists

Upstairs there are several ghosts. Firstly, there is one of an irate Victorian gentleman in his 70s with a stoop. He is alleged to have fallen down the staircase after suffering a stroke or being poisoned. Visitors often experience a dizzy light-headed sensation in this area, which is attributed to his ghost.

Secondly, two ghostly ladies haunt the upper floor. One is an unhappy ghost dressed in yellow, the other is dressed in blue. The Blue Lady has been seen materializing from a column of light in the room now known as the blue bedroom, where she has also been seen looking out of the bedroom window.

Another bedroom houses the phantom of a lady holding a monkey. She was seen by a Second World War sergeant major who was billeted to Littledean. She allegedly woke him by slapping him across the face before disappearing before his eyes.

There are also tales of a grisly ghost that is said to be the spirit of a deformed woman who was trapped in a windowless room at the top of the house. As her room could only be reached by a ladder and trapdoor, she was effectively imprisoned. A visiting psychic sensed her spirit and rescued her from the confines of her chamber.

In Donald's own bedroom he was woken one night by something stabbing him in the back. Minutes later he was pushed right across the bed. On another night he experienced a dark figure walking around an upstairs bedroom, but in the inky blackness was unable to see what it looked like.

Inexplicable smells are often noticed in the house. The smell of fresh toast can often be experienced in the east wing at 2pm, while the scent of sweet roses can be smelt even when there are no roses around. However, it seems the poltergeist who lives here dislikes flowers: a former housekeeper became so accustomed to finding flower displays thrown all over the floor that she gave up arranging them.

Above: *The phantom of a small black boy dressed in a red robe, and carrying a candle is the most prevalent ghost at Littledean Hall.*

Tragedy Strikes

The most well-known ghost at Littledean Hall is that of a young black servant who murdered his master in 1741, a story that historical records support. Charles Pyrke's servant and companion from an early age was a black child who had been brought to Littledean from one of the Pyrke family's sugar plantations in the West Indies. The pair grew up experiencing all of life's adventures together. But that was to come to an abrupt end one fateful day in 1741.

At the age of 23, Charles repeatedly raped the servant's sister. Eventually, she got pregnant and a child was born. It was a disgrace to the Pyrke family, so they had it killed and its body was hidden behind the wooden panelling in a bedroom. In an act of vengeance the servant murdered his master and now his remorseful ghost roams the landings and hallways of the house.

Sightings describe him as wearing a red robe and carrying a candle, but there is also a strange report that details his disappearance from a painting. One day in 1989, a visitor who was keen to see the painting of Charles and his servant came to the hall. However, she was dismayed to see that the painting that she had thought portrayed both characters showed only Charles. After accepting her disappointment she explored the rest of the house. At the end of her visit she decided to take one last look at the picture. She could not believe her eyes as the form of the servant boy gradually appeared within the painting. As she watched, an icy cold chill filled the room.

The painting is indeed surrounded with mystery; it is difficult to photograph because blurred areas appear on the prints for no logical reason, sometimes so much so that they cause the images to appear to be in negative. The painting hangs in pride of place at Littledean – a haunted painting in a haunted house.

There are more ghosts at Littledean – a ghostly gardener sweeping up leaves on autumn afternoons, misty figures on the driveway, a condemned witch in the grounds, ghostly lights in empty rooms, a cloudy shadow near the kitchen, slamming doors, the sound of breathing in the dark, footfall on wood where there is only carpet and chatterings along deserted corridors – all of which give you the unmistakable sense that there are unseen people all around you.

You are never alone at Littledean Hall...

BRITAIN'S MOST HAUNTED HOTEL

ETTINGTON PARK HOTEL, WARWICKSHIRE, ENGLAND

The stately spires and turrets of Ettington Park reach up to the sky and form the dramatic outline of a haunted mansion, which is now a hotel. Documented in the Domesday book in 1086, this grand old house has been in the same family since before the Norman Conquest. And, although it has changed uses over the years, from a nursing home to a public school to a disco, it is still owned by the Shirley family, who, after a great fire in 1980, injected millions of pounds into its restoration and subsequent use as a luxury hotel.

Below: *Ettington Park in Warwickshire is now a luxury hotel where ghost hunters can combine investigations with creature comforts.*

As the stately pile rose from the ashes, so too did the ghosts. There are many non-paying residents of a spectral nature in the house and grounds. The first story concerns the haunted library. You would be forgiven for thinking that this room, filled with Gothic arches and walls lined with ornate bookcases, is still in use as a place of study and learning, but you would be wrong. The room forms the hotel's main bar and serves every drink imaginable, but these are not the only spirits in the room. The notorious 'haunted book' jumps off of one particular shelf and shoots into the room, landing open at the same page always. The book is *St Ronan's Well Volume 1* by Sir Walter Scott (1771–1832) and it opens at a page where this verse by William Wordsworth (1770–1850) is printed:

...A merry place, 'tis said, in days of yore;
But something ails it now – The place is cursed.

I have examined the book and there is no obvious reason for it to be the focus of a haunting. Perhaps the ghost in the library is using it to scare away nervous guests? Or perhaps the spirit has a wicked sense of humour, as has been suggested by the hotel management? Either way, the book has flown off the shelf at least six times in recent years.

The same ghost has also been known to play around with the bottles behind the bar. Late one night, after all the guests had retired to bed, the house manager and a colleague were talking in the library when suddenly a smashing and crashing noise came from behind them. The pair then watched in amazement as bottles of drink were flicked off the shelf by some unseen presence. The ghostly prankster knocked one of each type of drink onto the floor before ceasing its poltergeist-like behaviour.

Late-night Wanderings

Night seems to be the time for ghosts at Ettington Park, with most of the activity reported either very late at night or during the early hours of the morning. The head porter told me that the lift goes up and down of its own volition at night. In the small hours, when he is at reception, he has often heard the lift come down, the bell ring to announce that it has stopped and the doors open, but the lift is always empty – at least of human occupants.

There is a ghost here that is fond of playing a round

Below: *Ettington Park's Head Porter keeps a firm hold on the haunted book, which can, under normal circumstances, be found in the hotel's libary.*

Above and above right: *The Stour Suite at Ettington Park Hotel is home to a Grey Lady. On occasion, this phantom leaves the hotel suite and has been seen gliding up and down the hotel's main staircase.*

of snooker, too. One night, after the snooker balls were locked away in the billiards room for the night, along with the cues, the house manager returned to reception. But he had only been there a few moments when he heard the distinctive clack, clack sound of snooker balls knocking together. He rushed back to the billiards room to find three balls on the green baize. No-one had passed him, so he is certain that the activity was caused by one of the hotel's ghosts.

The Stour Suite Spirit

Of all the 48 bedrooms in the mansion, none has received so much paranormal attention as The Stour Suite. Here, the ghost of a Grey Lady was seen by a terrified guest who rushed down to reception in his dressing gown to tell how he had been washing his hair when he glanced in the mirror to see the reflection of a woman wearing a grey smock, ruff collar and cap sitting on the edge of the bath behind him.

The same spirit has been sighted on the main staircase of the hotel, where she appears to walk above the existing stairs. The description of her appearance is always the same. It is generally accepted that she is the ghost of a former serving maid who fell down the stairs and broke her neck. The Grey Lady is the only ghost to have been caught on camera here – following the fire in 1980, an American tourist visited the gutted mansion before it had re-opened. He decided to take some photographs of the exterior. When he developed his prints he found the clear image of a lady in period dress staring at the camera from the window that is now part of The Stour Suite.

The photograph has long since been lost, but was kept by the hotel management for some years. Those who have seen it are convinced it is the spirit of the Grey Lady.

Crying Children

The saddest tale at Ettington concerns the ghosts of

two young children whose gravestones can still be seen in the grounds of the house. They lived in the village of Old Ettington, which was once located on the site of the current hotel. The church tower and a stone cross that marked the centre of the village are all that now remains of the village, which was abandoned when the villagers were forced to relocate 1½ miles (2.5km) away by the Master of Ettington when he enclosed the present park in 1795. In the shadow of the tower runs the River Stour, in which the two children are believed to have met a sad fate by drowning while playing innocently by the riverside one day.

In recent years, a couple from Hampshire stayed at the hotel in a bedroom that overlooks the meadows leading down to the river. During the night the woman was woken by the sound of children crying. She went to the window from where she saw the silhouettes of a young boy and girl staring up at her in the moonlight before disappearing into the night. Rubbing her eyes she put it down to her imagination and returned to bed.

The following night, after returning to their home in Hampshire she was again woken by the sound of crying children, but this time the sound seemed to be all around her. The phenomenon recurred on several occasions before she sought help from a vicar who advised her to return to the hotel to break the spell. After contacting Ettington Park and explaining the situation the hotel invited the couple back as their guests and they accepted readily, staying in the same room as before. The night passed without incident and she has never heard the children again.

Above: *The church tower is all that remains of Old Ettington village decades after the villagers were forced to relocate by a powerful member of the Shirley family.*

Chambermaids at the hotel tell of whispering voices in bedrooms and of windows opening and closing without the aid of human hands. Receptionists hear a tapping on the top of the reception desk but when they answer there is no one there. The sound of heavy footfall has been heard parading along the Long Gallery, but it does not worry the staff or most of the guests, for it is just another part of the ghostly tapestry of Ettington Park Hotel – the most haunted hotel in Britain.

Right: *The graves of two children can be seen in the hotel grounds, as may their ghosts.*

BRITAIN'S MOST HAUNTED INN

THE HIGHWAYMAN INN, SOURTON, DEVON, ENGLAND

The Highwayman Inn has to be seen to be believed. It is pure fantasy – part pirate ship, part church, part museum and part junk shop. Created over a period of 40 years by the talented John 'Buster' and Rita Jones, the building is now in the hands of John's daughter, Sally, and son-in-law, Bruce Thompson. Standing on the main highway through the village of Sourton, it attracts visitors from all over the world, many returning time after time to experience its unique and mysterious atmosphere.

An Auspicious Site

The site of the inn dates back to 1282 and is situated close to a ley line. Over the centuries it has changed hands and been renamed many times. When Buster and Rita took it over on Michaelmas Day, 1959, Rita renamed it The Highwayman. Indeed there were three known highwayman at large in the area at one time.

The current building comprises three wonderful main public rooms: the Coach Cabin Lounge, the Hideaway Bar and the Galleon Room. The interiors are fashioned from an eclectic collection of lanterns, brassware, Gothic arches from a church in Plymouth, a wooden door from a ship wreck, beams from a derelict cottage, cartwheels, stuffed animals and great tree trunks hauled from the peat bogs on nearby Dartmoor. Not surprisingly, with so many different artefacts from so many places, some have brought with them more than Buster and Rita bargained for and today the building is alive with ghostly activity, ranging from spectral footfall to full apparitions.

Samuel the Cavalier

The primary ghost at the inn is that of Samuel the Cavalier, who has been seen by Rita and many visitors, psychic and otherwise. On one occasion, he walked

Below: *The strange and unique Highwayman Inn attracts visitors not only for its local ales, but also for its ghosts.*

through a wall where a door used to lead to the old stable block. Descriptions of the friendly spirit of Sam, as he has been affectionately nicknamed, all tally, and he always appears in green with a large feather in his hat.

Sally believes Sam was connected with the Battle of Sourton Cross, which took place a mile away during the English Civil War (1642–9). Sightings of the spirit vary, but he often seems to appear at around 10am in the Galleon Room.

A few years ago, an eight-year-old child amazed her parents when she told them that she had talked to a man in a big hat with a feather in it, as the parents were well aware that there was no one in the Coach Cabin Lounge where she had been playing and no explanation could be found for her statement other than that she had been having a conversation with a ghost!

Evidence Abounds

There are other ghosts at The Highwayman too: a licentious woman in a mop cap, a man identified by a medium as Joseph who sits at the bar and a sea captain named Grenville. There is also another figure in a dark coat who came into the pub one day in 2002, causing the doorbell to ring as he entered, but he then walked into one of the bars and disappeared.

Video footage taken in the Galleon Room has captured orbs coming out of the door of the shipwreck of *The Diana*, which went down in 1817, taking 16 souls with it.

Photographs have shown anomalous images and séances have produced evidence of contact with the spirits of those that haunt this strange building, as well as suggestions of buried treasure on the site. There are also first-hand testimonies from countless witnesses who have seen and felt strange things at the inn and at Cobweb Hall across the road, which was originally Sourton's Victorian church hall but is now part of the inn and let out as a holiday home.

Here, in the magical interiors of The Highwayman, nothing else seems to exist. It's as if there is no world outside, as if all that matters is in there with you, from times past to times present. The Highwayman Inn is undoubtedly the most haunted inn in Britain.

Right: *This door was rescued from the shipwrecked* The Diana *and is now a focus of ghostly activity at the inn.*

BRITAIN'S MOST HAUNTED CASTLE

PENGERSICK CASTLE, PRAA SANDS, CORNWALL

Pengersick Castle today is a large pele tower which was once part of a much larger dwelling whose exact age is unknown. There is evidence of an apothecary's garden on the site during the 13th century, and this suggests that there was an earlier habitation here before the construction of the fortified manor house, or castle, which was built around 1500. There may have been a building here even earlier than the garden, as a manor on the site is mentioned in a document dated 1199 concerning a dispute over land ownership, and there are even suggestions of a Stone or Bronze Age settlement within the curtilage of the current castle.

Below: *Pengersick Castle at Praa Sands is one of Cornwall's haunted hotspots.*

Defying Rational Explanation

Over recent years much paranormal research has been conducted at Pengersick Castle, and its name has become synonymous with tales of ghosts and hauntings. The current owner is Angela Evans who, with her son, is enthusiastically restoring the castle and its grounds. While some of the paranormal findings are dubious, there is much at Pengersick that defies rational explanation. I, personally, have witnessed strange things in the castle which rattled even my objective veneer...

The tales begin with Henry and Engrina Pengersick whom, while they never lived in the building here today, are said to haunt it. Their home was Pengersick Manor, the building that stood here prior to the 16th-century building. Their haunting of the tower is said to be because stones used to build the castle were taken from the old manor house, thus introducing the ghosts to their new haunting ground.

The tower itself, as well as the surrounding buildings that have long since perished, was built during the reign of John Milliton. Legend has it that John was a wicked man who dabbled in black magic and practised his sorcery inside the pele tower. This is probably no more than a romantic exaggeration of the truth, as he is said to have tried to poison a troublesome wife; however, she suspected his plan and switched wine goblets, poisoning him instead. The ghost of John Milliton is now among the spectral company that haunts the building.

The Haunted Bedroom

The most haunted room in the tower is a bedroom with an old four-poster bed. The bed seems to be a catalyst for much of the supernatural activity that is reported in the room. Two ghosts are directly associ-

Above: *The haunted bedroom at Pengersick Castle is at the centre of the castle tower's paranormal activity.*

ated with the bed itself. The first is that of a young lady whose form manifests on the bed beneath spectral covers, while the second is the gaunt phantom of a woman who bends over to examine those who dare to sleep in the bed.

The room is the most atmospheric in the building and it exudes a weird otherworldly atmosphere which is sensed by many people.

Spectral Charm

I myself have witnessed the strange effect the castle has on people. During the daylight hours I had no problem exploring the rooms of the castle alone, but at night it was quite a different matter. Upon entering the haunted bedroom I was struck with fear, and failed to talk myself into staying alone in the chamber. Although I saw and heard nothing, there was undoubtedly a different feeling in the room. I can only describe it as a 'thick' and 'dark' atmosphere.

Those who do manage to stay long enough in the bedroom may encounter the legendary phantom of a black dog with fiery red eyes, which is said to be a demon trapped in the fireplace. I set a video camera up to observe this area of the room on Hallowe'en in 2001 and caught some orbs emanating from the stonework, but alas, no hound from Hell!

Ghost hunters come from far and wide to experience the spectral charm of the place and organized ghost watches are now held on a frequent basis. During one ghost watch some video footage showing a peculiar anomaly was recorded. The video appears to show several scampering ghost rats. I have examined the footage and cannot explain it. Several photographs showing different stages of ghost manifestation have also been taken, which also defy logical explanation.

Benign Presences?

Not all the ghosts at Pengersick are frightening. The most frequently seen spectre is that of a 14th-century monk in a black robe. Angela informed me that he has been seen mostly in the gardens, and that his activities seem focused on a stone archway in the grounds.

During my visit in 2001 I, too, saw a figure that appeared to be dressed in a dark robe in this area of the gardens, but I assumed it to be one of the team playing a practical joke. It wasn't! Upon further examination the figure had disappeared, and remains unexplained to this day. Some have suggested that this spirit is a monk from Hailes Abbey who was refused his tithes by Henry Pengersick in 1330.

The last spirit at the castle is that of a young girl who has been sighted on the battlements at the top of the tower. She danced to her death by falling inadvertently off the top of the tower and now delights in influencing visitors to do the same.

There are several other castles with a larger range of ghosts than Pengersick, but none with quite the same extraordinary track record for supernatural happenings. Therefore, it deserves the title of Britain's Most Haunted Castle.

BRITAIN'S MOST HAUNTED VILLAGE

PRESTBURY, GLOUCESTERSHIRE, ENGLAND

Just 5 miles (8km) from the Georgian town of Cheltenham in Gloucestershire lies the rural village of Prestbury. Prestbury means 'fortified settlement of the priests' and it has existed as a dwelling place since Anglo-Saxon times. Many foul deeds have taken place here, giving rise to a plethora of ghoulish and ghostly tales. The village also lies on a ley line, adding yet more ghosts to the area.

NB: Some of Prestbury's ghosts have either been exorcised or have had exorcism attempts made upon them and, therefore, they are not all still active.

Cleeve Hill
Ghostly Victorian Funeral Cortège

The first of the Prestbury hauntings is in the Cleeve Hill area. One light summer evening a teacher was returning by car to Cheltenham and was driving along Southam Road towards Prestbury. As she approached the village she noticed a funeral cortège in the field to her left. The party appeared to be a Victorian affair, with plumed black horses and a parade of mourners in black dress. It occurred to her that this was extremely odd in this day and age, and being an inquisitive sort of person she turned into Noverton Lane, turned the car round and went back up to Cleeve Hill along Southam Road. She was surprised to see no trace of the cortège or any of the people; they had simply vanished.

Below: *A ghostly Victorian funeral cortège has been seen making its way along Cleeve Hill before vanishing into thin air.*

Noverton Lane
Psychic Echoes

Inexplicable sounds emanate from the general area of Noverton Lane. These have been described as gruff voices accompanied by iron wheels on gravel. This strange occurrence regularly commences at 2am, when it pierces the silence of an otherwise peaceful country lane.

The High Street
The Woman in a Mob Cap

Some years ago a young man on a motorcycle passed through Prestbury along the High Street. As he turned the corner from Southam Road onto the High Street he came face to face with a woman crossing the road. She wore long clothes and a mob cap and seemed to be walking across the road a couple of feet below the present surface of the ground. The rider had to brake so sharply he was thrown off his bike and was mildly injured. On immediate inspection of the area the woman had vanished.

Idsall House

Idsall House is an imposing town mansion that is now used as the prestigious offices for a solicitors' firm. There are two ghosts at Idsall House.

The Attractive Ghost

The first ghost is that of a beautiful woman who has

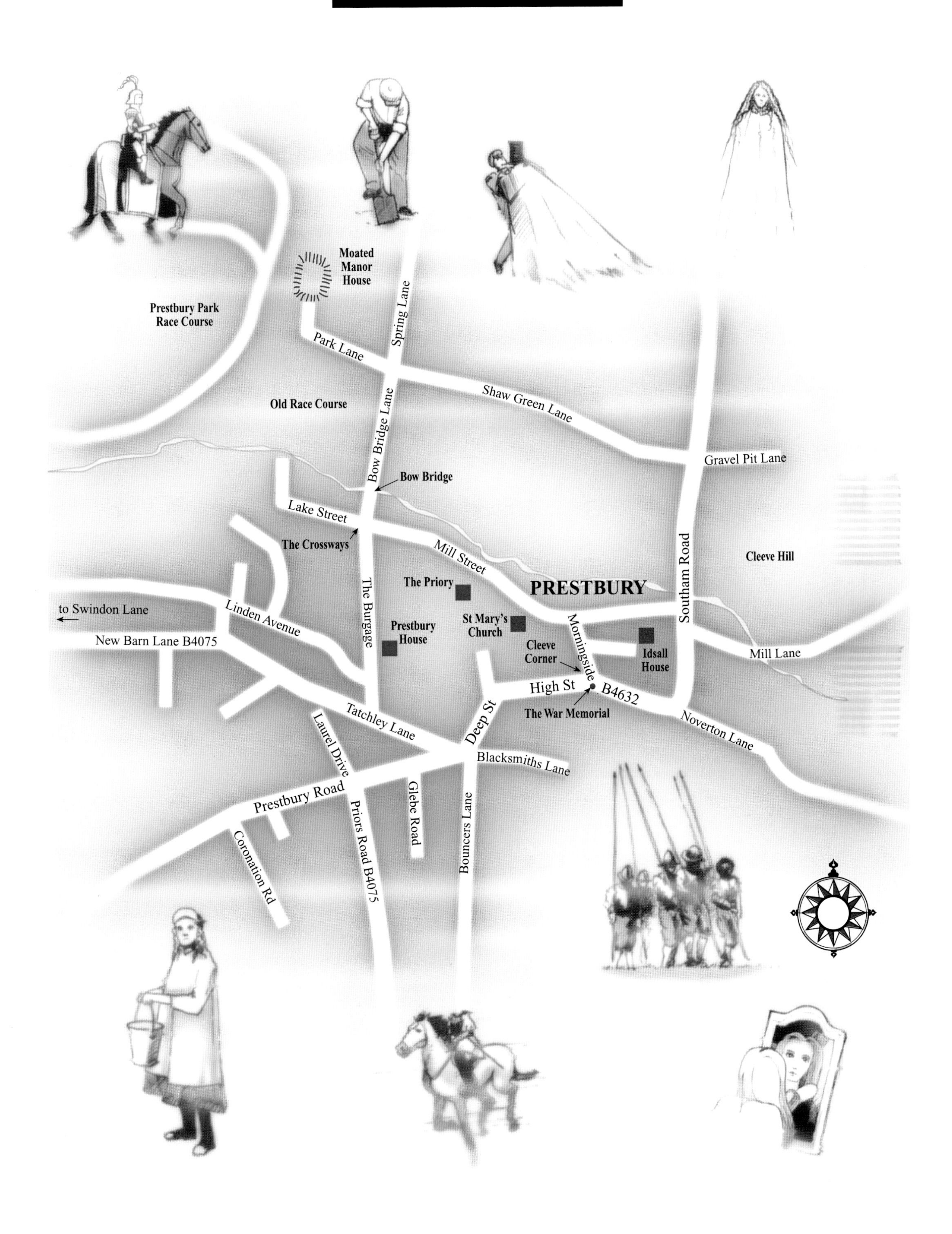
Moated Manor House
Prestbury Park Race Course
Spring Lane
Park Lane
Old Race Course
Bow Bridge Lane
Shaw Green Lane
Gravel Pit Lane
Bow Bridge
Lake Street
The Crossways
Mill Street
Cleeve Hill
Southam Road
The Priory
PRESTBURY
to Swindon Lane
Linden Avenue
New Barn Lane B4075
The Burgage
Prestbury House
St Mary's Church
Morningside
Idsall House
Mill Lane
Cleeve Corner
High St
B4632
The War Memorial
Tatchley Lane
Deep St
Noverton Lane
Laurel Drive
Blacksmiths Lane
Prestbury Road
Glebe Road
Priors Road B4075
Bouncers Lane
Coronation Rd

Above: *The Phantom Strangler resides in a bedroom at Cleeve Corner.*

been seen combing her hair in a mirror. Whether she is a spectre from the past or the present is unknown.

The Pushing Ghost

The second ghost at Idsall House haunts the basement, where it pushes people from behind. The man who experienced this ghostly push was alone in the basement at the time, although he does not intend to return there alone again.

In the past, there may have been another ghost at Idsall House, as it is recorded that when the building was a privately owned house, one member of the family refused to enter certain parts of the upper floors in case they met 'the apparition'.

Cleeve Corner
The Phantom Strangler

The tale of Cleeve Corner records a thief who broke into a bride's bedroom in an attempt to steal her dowry. However, the thief accidentally woke the bride and proceeded to strangle her to death with his bare hands before making off with his loot.

This gruesome murder is often given as a possible explanation for the paranormal incidents that have taken place in the room. Witnesses tell of waking in the dead of night feeling an all-pervading sense of dread and evil fill the room. Others tell of an unearthly light glowing from the window or of a 'cold and clammy' atmosphere.

The most unfortunate witnesses, however, run the risk of being strangled themselves, as the ghost has been known to attempt to strangle some who dared to sleep in the room. Those who have survived the experience have described 'feeling a terrible pressure on the throat which grows tighter and tighter' and it is said that only by gasping out a prayer will the phantom strangler recoil to the afterworld.

Another version of this tale suggests that the phantom strangler might be the bride's groom, who may have murdered his new wife and fled with the dowry.

High Street
The Singing Spectre

During the late 1950s and early 1960s it was reported that a cottage on the High Street was haunted by a singing ghost. Apparently, the clear sound of its singing became a regular occurrence during those years, but it has not been heard since.

The Lady in a Big Hat

The benign ghost of a little old lady haunts a house on Prestbury's High Street. She appears wearing a very large hat and walks between the kitchen and bedroom before vanishing.

The Peeping Lady

This nosy spectre makes scheduled, or cyclic, appearances on certain nights throughout the year. Details of which nights she appears is unclear, but the behaviour of the ghost is constant. The Peeping Lady emerges from the doorway of a house on the High Street and

makes her way along the road, peering into every available window as she goes. She has been described as wearing clothes of an ancient time. After satisfying her curiosity she returns the way she came and disappears into one of the almshouses, which date back to 1720.

The Poltergeist

According to the proprietor of a shop on the High Street the building houses a poltergeist, which on several successive nights saw fit to remove items from a small storeroom situated at the back of the building and deposit them in a pile in the middle of the main shop floor. It seems that this peculiar behaviour has pacified the poltergeist, as no further phenomena have been reported.

The Shadowy Figure

The proprietor of the same shop where the poltergeist has been reported also tells of a second presence. On occasions a black shadowy figure has been seen gliding across a room above the shop. Why this phantom shadow should haunt is unknown, but it may be that it is the same ghost as is active downstairs.

Above: *Many of the buildings on Prestbury's High Street are haunted.*

The Phantom Jockey

One evening in the 1970s, four young women were walking along the High Street when they saw a man standing opposite The King's Arms inn waiting to cross the road. By the dim light of the street lamp nearby they noticed that he was wearing a jockey's clothes, including breeches, racing blouse and a peaked cap. He started to cross the road but, to their amazement, he vanished into thin air before reaching the centre of the road. After turning the corner into Deep Street they were even more amazed to see the same man give a repeat performance of his disappearing act.

It is no surprise that one of Prestbury's ghosts is that of a jockey, as the village has strong horse-racing connections. But why he should manifest on a street pavement is not known. Perhaps he is re-enacting a moment of importance in his life? Or possibly he was killed by being run over?

Above: *The graveyard of St Mary's Church is haunted on occasion by the Black Abbot – Prestbury's most famous ghost – and by a lady dressed in white.*

The Spectral Motorcyclist

According to Peter Underwood in his book *Ghosts And How To See Them*, a ghostly young male motorcyclist haunts Prestbury's High Street. Who he is and why he haunts, as with so many other of Prestbury's ghosts, is unknown.

Deep Street
The Hurrying Monk

No. 10 Deep Street is a modern bungalow, and perhaps the last place you would expect to find a ghost, but both here and in The Thatched Bakery (the thatched cottage on the corner of Deep Street and High Street) people have seen the ghost of a hurrying monk.

The Black Abbot

This ghost is probably the best known in the entire village as he has been written about countless times. Exactly why an abbot should haunt the village is not clear, but it may have something to do with Prestbury's ancient history. It is believed that the gardens of what is now called Reform Cottage on Deep Street were used as burial grounds for the Prior of Llanthony's 'cannon's regular' – those priests living under rule. It is also known that the house that stands immediately next to Reform Cottage was used as a mortuary. Perhaps this is why the Black Abbot is seen wandering around Reform Cottage and its garden.

Traditionally, the Black Abbot makes three anniversary visits per year – at Easter, on All Saints Day and at Christmas. He is said to begin his walk on each of these occasions in the churchyard of St Mary's Church. He then walks through the grounds of The Priory to emerge in Deep Street, where he walks along the roadside path to Reform Cottage.

Previous owners of Reform Cottage have become quite accustomed to their spectral visitor. They have often heard his footsteps as he bumps and bangs around the upstairs rooms after his walk.

Past owners were aware of his presence, too. One couple from London decided to convert the barn next to the cottage into a living area and put in a floor to divide up the building. One of the workmen said he had felt as if he was being watched by an unseen presence. The completion of the work was marked by the ghostly abbot, who threw a large plant pot at the wall. It landed between the head workman and the owner!

Those who have seen the Black Abbot are surprised at how real he looks – until he disappears. On one occasion the ghost appeared in the middle of the road, causing a motorcyclist to swerve violently – almost causing a tragic accident. At other times he has been seen inside the church itself, although it has apparently been exorcized now, which may explain why he no longer appears inside. The exorcism doesn't seem to prevent him taking an interest in what goes on around the churchyard, however, and many people say they have seen him there after funerals.

The last known haunt of the Black Abbot is the churchyard steps that lead down to Mill Street. He has been sighted here on several occasions, normally in the early morning at around 6am. Perhaps it is because of his presence on these steps that horses and, sometimes, dogs refuse to go past the spot?

The Civil War Soldiers

The cottage called The Old House on Deep Street has been the site of several curious paranormal manifestations, and one family who lived here in the early 1990s had a particularly unusual encounter. Their four-year-old son complained that he did not want to be left alone in the kitchen while his mother was in another part of the house. On being asked why, he proclaimed that he did not like the soldiers who came in.

Below: *The grounds of The Priory are also haunted by Prestbury's famous Black Abbot.*

Above: *The Three Queens was once the haunt of a ghost named Mrs Brown.*

'What soldiers?', asked his mother in amusement. 'Funny soldiers with boots up to here', he said, indicating his thigh, 'and with big hats.'

The child was far too young to know anything of Prestbury's history relating to the English Civil War (1642–9), and couldn't possibly have known that a skirmish had taken place on just the other side of the kitchen wall where he claimed to have seen the figures.

The Ghost Lights

The figures in the kitchen are not the only phenomena to have occurred at Deep Street's The Old House. Tenants past and present have told of strange and inexplicable lights shining in various parts of the building. A recent resident of the building stated that accounts of the 'ghost lights' go back many, many years, some as far as his grandfather's occupancy of the house. Light phenomena are often reported at haunted sites, and are believed to be the first stage of a manifesting entity.

The Ghostly Vicar

The large old house called The Three Queens on the corner of Deep Street and Tatchley Lane is home to the ghost of a former vicar. His apparition has been seen in the hall and in the study in which he used to prepare his sermons. The ghost is a benign shade who has been heard to proclaim, 'A man's work is never done!', while rubbing his hands together.

The house has been named The Three Queens because sections of it were built during the reigns of Queen Elizabeth I (1533–1603), Queen Anne (1665–1714) and Queen Victoria (1837–1901). The building was used as a vicarage for many years, but is now a private house.

The Ghost of Mrs Brown

Another ghost of The Three Queens was that of a Mrs Brown. When the late Canon Urling Smith lived in the building, inexplicable noises were a regular occurrence. He wasn't bothered by the ghost, however, and told any disturbed visitors, 'Do not worry, it's only Mrs Brown!' However, when his son became ill and was brought to live in the house, Mrs Brown's presence seemed to prevent his recuperation and so an exorcism was carried out. This was apparently successful as she has not been heard since.

Bouncers Lane
The Glowing Gardener

Accounts of a glowing figure have been given by many Prestbury residents. According to those who have seen him, this ghost appears during the hours of darkness, apparently tending to one of the allotments on Bouncers Lane as he is seen bending over, as if digging.

Swindon Lane
The Phantom Shepherd

The account of a ghostly shepherd on Swindon Lane dates from one foggy night in 1975 when the phantom was seen meandering along the lane accompanied by a herd of sheep. No explanation was forthcoming for the apparitions, all of which disappeared into the fog, and no further occurrences have ever been reported.

The Burgage
The Old Man with a White Beard

Above: *Prestbury House Hotel has many ghostly tales attached to it and, therefore, offers perfect accommodation for a ghost hunter.*

According to many references, the Prestbury House Hotel has a ghost. Despite this, the hotel's literature claims, 'There are no ghost stories about the inside of the hotel'.

However, several accounts of Prestbury's various ghosts state that there is a room in the hotel that is boarded up and never used because it is believed to be haunted. In the 1950s, a housekeeper reported to a local carpenter that she had heard strange noises coming from the boarded-up room.

Following a change of ownership, several major alterations were made to the building, including the addition of a water tank in the haunted room. Two plumbers were enlisted to carry out the installation, but they fled before the work was completed, claiming that they had encountered an apparition of an old man dressed in white with a long white beard. However, they had not been terrified by the sudden appearance of the ghost as much as by its threatening behaviour. The ghost is alleged to have shouted 'Get out, get out of here!', while brandishing a big stick. The plumbers refused to complete the job, threatening resignation if their foreman forced them to return.

It is not unusual for building alterations to disturb otherwise dormant hauntings, and this seems to have been the case with this particular ghost.

The history of the Prestbury House Hotel suggests that the ghost may be that of one of the Capel family who lived in the building until 1964. The Capel in question was first held prisoner in a small garret when Oliver Cromwell's men seized the house. He was later beheaded on The Burgage, right outside Prestbury House Hotel, for his loyalty to Charles I (1600–1649). Could it be his ghost that now haunts the tiny upstairs room, and that this is possibly the one in which he was held prisoner?

The Servant Girl

This spectre is of a beautiful servant girl carrying a water pitcher. Her clothing suggests that she has haunted this land since ancient times, and long before a house ever stood on these grounds. She has been seen standing in the gardens on several occasions.

The Visiting Horseman

Occasional accounts of a ghostly horseman are given at Prestbury House Hotel. The sounds of a horse clattering into the courtyard and stables area, followed by human footsteps walking into the house have been witnessed. These phenomena seem to be unconnected to the village's three other ghostly riders.

The Headless Dispatch Rider

Of Prestbury's three spectral horsemen, this is perhaps the most famous. Legend has it that a Royalist dispatch rider was making the journey from Sudeley Castle near Winchcombe to Gloucester carrying important documents relating to the English Civil War (1642–9). During this time, The Burgage was occupied by Parliamentary Roundheads. They had set in place a rope across the road which, when pulled taut, caused the galloping horse to stumble and fall, delivering the unfortunate rider and his dispatches into enemy hands. The rider was immediately killed by the Roundheads, who decapitated him. The horse galloped away, riderless.

Above: *A medieval messenger clatters around the area known as The Crossways, where his skeleton was unearthed.*

Many residents of the village claim to have heard or seen The Headless Dispatch Rider, some hearing the sound of a horse galloping past at speed, others describing the sound of a horse's hooves followed by a sudden pause and then more sounds of hooves.

In the early 1970s, a sighting of this ghost, accompanied by sounds, was experienced at the junctions of Deep Street, Blacksmiths Lane and Bouncers Lane. The witnesses described a vague misty outline of a horse mounted by a headless rider.

Others have heard this ghost galloping along Shaw Green Lane and Bow Bridge Lane. However, it's favourite haunt appears to be The Crossways area, where some residents are said to dash outside each time they hear the horse's hooves, only to find there is nothing there to account for what they have heard.

The Spinet Player

Sundial Cottage was built in 1672 and is home to Prestbury's most gentle ghost. The haunting here is of spectral music and takes the form of the ghostly sounds of a spinet being played. The sound has been heard many times, normally during the summer months and particularly during the evening. There are conflicting stories explaining the haunting of Sundial Cottage.

The first states that the ghost is that of a professor of music who used to teach pupils in the room from which the ghostly music sometimes emanates. The second tale tells of a young girl who plays the spinet in the garden. Indeed, the sound has been heard coming from outside rather than inside on many occasions. It has even been heard by people on the adjoining housing estate.

One account also tells of a sighting of a young girl on the upstairs landing of the house. The story goes that it is the ghost of a young girl who was forbidden to marry the man she loved and was confined to Sundial Cottage. She consoled herself by playing the spinet. On quiet summer evenings her music can still be heard wafting along The Burgage, but the visual aspect of the haunting rarely manifests now.

One particularly convincing account of this haunting is given by a mother who fled from the bombs of London during the Second World War (1939–45) to live at Sundial Cottage with her 12-year-old son. After a short time the child became irritable and lost his appetite. When asked what was wrong, he told his mother that he couldn't sleep at night because of the 'funny music'. Puzzled by this, his mother swapped bedrooms with him and she too heard the 'funny music'. It was only after this that she learned the story of the spectral spinet player.

Old Moses

Beautiful Walnut Cottage, originally a coach house that has now been converted into a private home, is alleged to have a visiting ghost. This presence seems to be harmless, and is even friendly enough to identify itself if asked. In 1961, the resident of Walnut Cottage, along with five other people, encountered the ghost in the dining room. They challenged it and it replied, 'Here's Old Moses! You see I likes to look in sometimes.'

A second ghostly incident is recorded as having taken place in the dining room, but this time during dinner. The owner at the time was discussing the subject of ghosts and let it be known in no uncertain terms that he could never believe in them, at which point a large mirror inexplicably flew off the wall and landed with a crash on the floor.

Is Old Moses a villainous former racehorse owner as has been suggested? Or is he the spectre of an 18th-century groom who once lived in the building? We shall never know for sure.

Above: *The haunting sound of a ghostly spinet player is heard in and around Sundial Cottage.*

The Crossways
The Medieval Messenger

On misty spring mornings the faint clattering of a horse's hooves accompanied by the apparition of a rider on a white horse may be witnessed in this area of the village. The ghost is thought to be that of a medieval messenger dating from 1471, who was perhaps a rider journeying to Edward IV's camp at Tewkesbury. While passing through Prestbury, he was allegedly shot down by a single arrow. The latest reported sighting of the messenger dates from 1989.

An interesting twist in this tale occurred some years ago when road improvements were being undertaken on Shaw Green Lane. The workers stumbled upon a skeleton which, when examined, was found to have an arrow between its ribs...

The Knight on Horseback

This spectral horseman appears as a knight in armour who, in contrast with Prestbury's other ghostly riders, pauses and salutes before galloping off into the distance.

Mill Street
The Shining Man

One of Mill Street's many spectral inhabitants has become known as The Shining Man due to his alarming appearance.

During one dark night in 1982, a young lad found himself alone in Mill Street. He had been out with some friends but they were walking way ahead of him. On turning a corner, he saw a car coming towards him, and in the glare of its headlights he saw a figure making its way along the path in front of him, going in the same direction. In a few moments he had caught up with the figure and was about to make his way round it when the figure weaved in front of him, preventing him from passing.

The lad noticed that the figure wore a long fawn-coloured overcoat and that it seemed not to have any legs beneath the coat! He attempted to speak to the figure in order to get past. On being spoken to the figure turned to show that it had no face. It then held up its hand and a light, as of that from a torch, shone out from its palm. Immediately following this action the ghostly figure turned and vanished into thin air.

The Phantom Tea Party

Before the Second World War (1939–45), a family from Cheltenham were trying to buy a pony for their young

Above: *The churchyard of St Mary's Church is still haunted by the ghostly Black Abbot, even though his spirit was exorcised from visiting the building itself.*

daughter and heard there was one for sale at Prestbury House. So, they visited one Sunday afternoon to see the animal. Prestbury House was then owned by one Major Capel, who enthusiastically showed off the pony to the potential purchasers.

Becoming bored very quickly, the young girl ventured off in the direction of the old stables, which were situated near Mill Street, a short walk across a field. She was delighted to find tables of people in old-fashioned dress having a party and she stayed for a moment to watch them.

None of them seemed to pay any attention to her and so she ran back to her mother saying, 'Mummy, come and see the fancy-dress party.' At the child's insistence that she follow, the mother reluctantly went with her daughter towards the stables. The daughter could see that the party was getting out of hand, there was shouting and rowdiness, but to the child's astonishment her mother scolded her saying, 'You are a very naughty girl for saying you could see a fancy-dress party.'

Unable to forget her peculiar experience, the girl returned to Prestbury 30 years later and located the site of the party she had seen. Research has since proved that in the late 17th and early 18th centuries a grotto had existed on this spot. In those days it was a place of merriment and partying. By 1819 the building had become an inn and had gained a reputation as a place of ill-repute. In 1859, the owner of Prestbury House bought the inn and closed it down because it had become noisy and attracted the wrong crowd, especially at weekends.

It was on a Sunday afternoon that the young child had witnessed the rowdy party. Had she glimpsed something from the distant past that had slipped momentarily into her present?

The Stick Lady

This friendly ghost appears as a little old lady who goes about her business collecting small sticks from the roadside down Mill Street. The Stick Lady seems to favour the locality of a particular cottage on Mill Street, as she has been seen passing by its windows on several occasions. It has been suggested that the reason she appears in front of the windows is that a path once ran in front of this particular cottage.

The Lady in White

The Lady in White is reputed to manifest in Mill Street, she then wanders across the street and glides into and around the churchyard. Her identity is unknown.

Ghost of Mrs Preece

According to the account, this apparition appears as a white misty form and glides across the fields towards Mill Street until it reaches a boundary wall where, after a little hesitation, it vanishes. Who it is and why it has become known as Mrs Preece cannot be traced.

The Marching Men

A local man was walking his dog along Mill Street one foggy night when he suddenly heard the sound of a group of marching men approaching him from the direction of Shaw Green Lane. The dog sank back on its haunches in an obvious state of terror and raised its hackles, but a few moments later the sound abruptly stopped. According to the reports, this strange phenomenon occurred again, although in a slightly different area but still near Shaw Green Lane. During the English Civil War (1642–9), Oliver Cromwell had a garrison in Prestbury House, so perhaps this marching sound is an echo of his troops.

The Phantom Horses

A former Prestbury postman has told of phantom horses on Mill Street. He used to begin his round very early in the morning and would often see horses from the village's racing stables being taken out for exercise. Hearing them coming down Mill Street he would move across to the church wall to allow them to pass and he would call a cheery greeting to the stable lads. However, on more than one occasion he heard horses trot past him but saw absolutely nothing.

Morningside House
The Leering Monk

A now-demolished Prestbury property known as Morningside House was once home to the ghost of a monk with an unpleasant leer who used to slide around the walls of the drawing room. It is possible that this ghost has departed Prestbury since the building was demolished or, perhaps, as with so many other ghosts, he will frequent whatever building stands on the same site in the future.

The Old Racecourse
The Cleeve Hill Ghost

Late one summer afternoon, two ladies were making their way along the path that leads from Cleeve Hill to the road next to the racecourse with the intention of making their way towards Aggs Hill. As they approached the racecourse gate they were surprised to see a man walking towards them as the path was normally deserted. When they reached the gate, however, the man seemed to have disappeared. There was nowhere he could have gone other than along the path, which they deemed impossible because they could see a long stretch of it, yet he was nowhere to be seen.

Later that afternoon the ladies bumped into the local vicar and recounted their strange encounter to him. He wasn't surprised, however, and told them that he had heard many accounts of people seeing The Cleeve Hill Ghost.

Below: *Mill Street is favoured as a haunting ground by several of Prestbury's otherworldly villagers.*

Favourite Old Haunts

THE WELLINGTON HOTEL, BOSCASTLE, CORNWALL

Set amid the historic village of Boscastle in Cornwall, the 16th-century Wellington Hotel is a popular place for locals and travellers alike. Boscastle is a magical place. It lies in a deeply wooded valley and its quaint slate-roofed buildings and Elizabethan harbour almost transport you back through time. It is no wonder, then, that Boscastle claims a grand ghostly heritage and that no building claims more ghost stories than 'The Welly', as it is affectionately known by the locals.

Ghostly encounters at the hotel are a common occurrence and, as its reputation as a haunted building has attracted many with a spiritual inclination, there have been many encounters recorded over recent years.

Below: *The Elizabethan harbour of Boscastle is just one historic element of this olde worlde English village that is home to the haunted Wellington Hotel.*

A Converted Non-Believer

Victor Tobutt was the owner of the hotel for some 16 years and, although he has since moved on, the legacy of his haunted hotel remains. Many years ago, Victor told me of his first experience of the building's ghostly guests and of his transformation from sceptic to believer. 'I was sitting counting the takings at reception one evening soon after we had taken on the hotel and as I looked up the stairs to the landing I saw a frock-coated figure move across the landing. He seemed to be wearing a ruffled shirt and leather gaiters, and his hair was tied back in a ponytail. From his appearance, I would guess he was a coachman of some sort, or maybe a stable lad.'

Following this strange sighting, Victor went down to the bar where Tom Gregory, who had been head barman at the hotel for some 20 years, told him that the figure had been seen many times before. In fact, Victor had hardly begun his description of the ghost before Tom knew exactly what he

Above: *The pretty Cornish coastal village of Boscastle is alive with stories of the dead, but nowhere in the village claims more supernatural heritage than the local hotel, The Welly.*

had seen. As a result of his experience, Victor now believes in ghosts. During the period he was in charge of the building he was to hear many more accounts of strange sightings and ghostly experiences.

Occupied Rooms

In the early 1990s, Bill Searle, a retired police officer was employed by the hotel as a general handyman and porter. No sooner had he settled into his new job than he had his first brush with the supernatural. On the tower landing, outside Rooms 15, 16 and 17, Bill distinctly saw the phantom of a young girl, which disappeared into windows that lead to the castellations of the tower. He was absolutely amazed by his experience, and as a down-to-earth kind of chap his testimony can be taken seriously. His second sighting was to follow 18 months later; again it was of the young girl and in exactly the same part of the hotel.

Another ghost in the building is that of a little old woman dressed in a black cloak who haunts Rooms 9 and 10. Guests had often commented that Room 10 was haunted, but it wasn't until Bill found a little old lady sitting on the end of the bed during one of his maintenance rounds that the claims were taken seriously.

More recently, chambermaid Debbie Jordan was checking the rooms when she saw an old lady go through the door of Room 9. Unaware that this room was let, she called the receptionist only to be told that no-one was staying in that room. It would appear that Debbie had seen the same ghost as Bill.

The next incident recorded in the paranormal archives of The Wellington Hotel took place in Spring 1996. A young man had been staying at the hotel and, being interested in all things ghostly, he enquired about the hotel's ghostly reputation. On hearing about Rooms 9 and 10, he asked the receptionist, Sandra Winstanley, if he might walk along the corridor that led to the haunted bedrooms. Upon his return he informed Sandra that, 'The little old lady in Room 10 is grateful that when you visited the room at 2.30pm you did not spend long there and did not disturb her.' Sandra was astonished because she always carried out her housekeeping checks at 2.30pm and never lingered in Room 10 because of its ghostly reputation!

BERRY POMEROY CASTLE, DEVON

Berry Pomeroy is a crumbling ruin of a castle, perched atop a crag, on the convergence of ley lines. It was abandoned in the late 17th century and now lies hidden in its haunted valley. For years it has been the site of countless encounters with the world beyond and deserves its reputation as a cold place of hauntings and of horrors.

Unfinished Business

The castle was originally built in the late 15th century as the family seat of the de Pomeroys, an ancient baronial family who came to Devon at the time of the Norman Conquest. In 1547 the castle was bought by the Seymour family, who proceeded to update the late medieval buildings with a more fashionable design, and the castle passed from heir to heir until it was abandoned, still incomplete, between 1688 and 1701.

After decades of decay, the castle fell into ruin and began to acquire its reputation for ghostly tales and legends. By the 18th century it was well established as a 'haunted castle'.

A common misconception held by many people is that ghosts are usually nocturnal, but this is not so at Berry Pomeroy. Most of the manifestations, which range from ice-cold patches of air, sightings, sounds, touchings, temporal possession, physical disablement and scents, occur both day and night at Berry Pomeroy. The only exception is the 'White Lady' – the spirit of Lady Margaret de Pomeroy – who is more often witnessed during the hours of darkness. She is clad from head to foot in a white dress and her wild hair blows behind her in the wind. Margaret is the sad sister of Lady Eleanor de Pomeroy. The two women were in love with the same man, so the jealous Eleanor imprisoned her sister in the deepest dungeon in the castle, where she eventually starved to death. Margaret's vengeful spirit is now one of Berry Pomeroy's most famous ghosts. She has frequently been seen along the rampart walk or in the lower cell of the tower, which is now known as St Margaret's Tower.

Another much more dreadful phantom at the castle is the Blue Lady. She is thought to be the ghost of a former daughter of a baron of Berry Pomeroy who had borne a child by her own father and subsequently killed it by strangling. Her aggrieved ghost has haunted the castle for at least the past 200 years, as her spirit was first recorded at the end of the 18th century. Sightings describe her as, 'Ringing her hands as if in anguish and with a look upon her face of great agony and remorse.' It is believed that a sighting of the Blue Lady heralds a death, as a family physician saw her ghost just prior to the death of a member of the family and other deaths have also followed her spectral visitations.

Bad Intentions

Ghost hunters should take special care at the castle for the Blue Lady often takes a distinct dislike to visitors. In 1913 a young army officer visited the castle while on leave. He saw a young woman bathed in a mysterious blue light, perched precariously on the ivy-clad walls, beckoning him. Assuming that she dare not move for fear of falling, he went to her aid. No sooner had he stepped onto the masonry than it fell away beneath his feet. It was a miracle that he avoided plunging to his death. Since then, the ghost has become renowned for luring those of weak minds and foolish natures to follow her onto the treacherous castle walls, a perilous activity and one that will almost certainly end in death.

The ghost of the Blue Lady is one of the most commonly reported sightings at the castle, and one account tells of a local who was foolish enough to visit during the hours of darkness. He and several friends watched in fear as a figure swathed in a blue aura formed in front of them in the main tower. Staring directly at them, the spectre said, 'Beware the hour, beware the hour', at which point they turned and fled. Minutes later it turned 11pm, and as they turned back to look at the castle they saw the windows turn a deep black and the great wooden gate begin to shake violently as if the castle itself was coming alive in some bizarre supernatural awakening.

Fearsome Fangs

The castle is the perfect subject for an artist, and one summer some years ago a lady called Aya Broughton decided to paint the romantic ruin of Berry Pomeroy. She had no idea about the castle's supernatural reputation and, although she was psychic, she initially sensed nothing and so set about her work in the courtyard. Nevertheless, she did experience something evil that day; something malevolent that meant her harm. It took the shape of a great black dog, which manifested in the courtyard and proceeded to stare at her with red, hateful eyes.

Being psychic, Aya knew this was an apparition and she noticed that while it was present the birds in the area seemed to flee and the light altered in such a way that the whole castle became illuminated as if some awful elemental power were flowing from the very stones in the walls. The thing came close to her, leering and with saliva drooling from its fangs. Struck with fear but with a deep determination that she must not show weakness she recited a prayer and continued with her painting. Gradually, the beast faded away and the castle returned to its normal appearance; she left soon after.

Fated lovers

The arbour is haunted by the ghosts of two lovers who met their untimely deaths here as the result of a bitter family feud in the 17th century. One of the lovers was from the de Pomeroy family, the other from a local family who owned nearby Darting Hall. The pair were discovered courting in the arbour and were brutally slain, but by which family still remains a mystery as both families disapproved of the romance.

The lovers' unhappy spirits have been witnessed

Below: *The crumbling ruins of Berry Pomeroy Castle stand majestically atop a rocky crag and are haunted by a plethora of ghosts.*

here many times, and they have even been caught on camera. The arbour is now known locally as The Ghost Walk, and visitors have reported strange encounters with a disembodied screeching and roaring entity which cannot be seen, only heard.

Travelling Torments

Other accounts describe the ghost of Henry de Pomeroy, one of the castle's founding fathers, who killed himself by blindfolding his horse and coaxing it over the edge of the cliff on which the castle sits, causing it to fall to its death and taking its rider with it into Gatcombe Valley, hundreds of feet below. Some say they have seen this strange suicide re-enacted and heard the psychic echo of the horse's master urging it over the cliff.

The melancholic sound of a child crying among the ruins has also been heard. Perhaps it is the sound of the Blue Lady's murdered child?

And then there is the record of a ghost hunter who met a black mass, which he described as 'the hugest, deepest, blackest thing I've ever seen. It was an evil entity.' He claims it followed him all the way home to his house in Paignton, Devon.

The same investigator managed to communicate with another ghost at the castle using a ouija board. It called itself Isabelle and appeared in a dress from the Restoration period (1660). The investigator recalls that, 'She struck us as a very evil little girl.' She told them that she was an illegitimate child of a disinherited member of the de Pomeroy family. The ghost hunter in question continued to be haunted by the little girl at his own home for some time, but his is not the only tale where the ghosts of the castle follow visitors when they leave.

Two other visitors who both took away pieces of the castle's stonework as unofficial souvenirs later returned them by post accompanied by letters describing frightening phenomena that had befallen them.

The ghost of an old man with a scythe has been reported outside the castle, as has an 'old lady in quaint, old fashioned garments' and even a 'cavalier with a large feathered hat, doublet and hose'. And an unpleasant-looking girl 'with smouldering black unwinking eyes which stared malignantly', who is dressed in a sack with a cord around her waist, has been seen nearby.

Another frequent phenomenon is that of inexplicable pockets of freezing cold air and sounds that defy rational explanation, including thuds, tramping feet, galloping horses' hooves and doors slamming.

The whole area seems to be subject to the jinx factor too, with camera malfunctions and all kinds of technical hitches occurring for no apparent reason.

One of the most noticeable aspects of the castle is its silence, which is accompanied by the sense that you are being watched. Many visitors comment on the sense of evil about the place, while others who have no prior knowledge of the site bluntly refuse to enter. Children are particularly sensitive to the dark forces here.

The spine-chilling aura of Berry Pomeroy Castle attracts ghost hunters from all over the world as it is a treasure chest of ghosts, timeslips and terrors. No ghost hunter can avoid it; it is a place that has to be experienced to be believed, and once visited will never be forgotten.

Below: *The gatehouse of Berry Pomeroy Castle houses a great door that has been shaken violently by a supernatural force.*

MARGELLS, BRANSCOMBE, DEVON

Built on the site of a 13th-century monastery, Margells is the oldest cottage in the Devonshire village of Branscombe and is now owned by the Landmark Trust. Its name derives from the late 1600s, when it was written 'Marckells', and it is part of an earlier building of Tudor origin.

The ghosts of Margells are led by a phantom monk now known as Brother Anselm. The monk's hauntings are well known throughout the village; they take many forms and have been documented for years.

A Haunted Holiday

In July 1992, two ladies spent a few days in the cottage, which is available to rent as a holiday home. They were disturbed one night at 2am by a loud swishing noise and a crashing noise, which was likened to the sound of a gun being fired at a metal bread bin, emanating from the kitchen. There was also a variety of other noises, including knockings and thumpings, none of which could be explained.

The most commonly reported phenomenon, however, is the sound of slow footfall in the upper rooms or on the wooden spiral staircase and the displacement of objects.

Bessie's Nightmare

There is a report from 1993 about a dog, Bessie, that was disturbed by ghostly antics. As dogs are not usually allowed upstairs in properties belonging to the Landmark Trust, Bessie had to sleep alone down-

Below: *Idyllic Margells is built on the site of a former monastery, which might explain the presence of a phantom monk known as Brother Anselm.*

Left: *Holidaymakers often sleep with the light on in the ancient cottage of Margells, one of the most haunted houses in Devon.*

stairs. In the middle of the night she began to wail frantically. Eventually, her awakened owner came downstairs to see what the matter was. The owner discovered that an earthenware jug had been placed upright in the middle of the dog's bed. Meanwhile, Bessie was howling in fear and staring blankly at the jug. For the rest of the night Bessie was allowed to sleep upstairs!

Smells and Sounds

Other visitors have reported inexplicable smells, such as the scent of incense and Stilton cheese, hearing the sound of a violin being played out of tune and the disconcerting echo of a ghostly monk chanting his rosary in the small screen bedroom – the most haunted room in the cottage.

The Visitors' Book

One entry in the visitors' book describes the strange apparition of a man with bandages round his head coming downstairs, while others refer to sightings of a ghost with the nickname of Ghostly Fred.

Local villagers remember hearing stories of a clock that would move itself from the mantelpiece in the drawing room to the floor without breaking and of sounds of spectral singers when there was no-one there.

Another, more poignant, entry in the visitors' book describes 'a rapping that could have awoken the dead. A deliberate rat-a-tat-tat of ancient knuckles on gnarled oak with a hearty deliverance. Brother Anselm is among us.' Another entry states, 'We could stay no longer – the ghost drove us out...'

John, deceased husband of actress **Bo Derek** still lingers to comfort his wife. Bo has witnessed the undeniable scent of honey butter, scones and turkey sausages wafting from the kitchen in the home they shared. Upon investigation there is nothing cooking to explain the smell. John's presence comforts Bo and she has said, 'John was the love of my life. I want him to haunt me forever.'

ATHELHAMPTON HALL, DORSET

The grand stately hall of Athelhampton was built by the Martyn family in 1485 on the site of the Bishop of Salisbury's manor and the legendary site of the palace of King Athelstan (895–939).

The house has been the focus of much psychic research and is among those considered the most haunted in Britain. The hall is open to the public, and those who visit frequently report ghostly encounters and strange experiences.

Five Phantoms

The records tell of five main ghosts at the hall. There are a pair of phantom Royalist duellists who are sighted in the Great Hall, and the house did have Royalist connections during the English Civil War (1642–9). After completing a ghostly duel the pair sit down to dinner at the table.

Athelhampton also has a Grey Lady; she has been seen drifting around the corridors and passageways of the older parts of the hall, but is most often seen in the State Bedroom – the most haunted room in the house. On one occasion a house guide asked her to leave, it being late in the afternoon and almost closing time, at which point she obediently arose from her chair, floated across the room and disappeared into the oak-panelled wall.

Another ghost is that of a monk or priest dressed in black robes who haunts the topiary gardens, but upon being approached he vanishes into thin air. There is some speculation that he may be the spirit of a former rector who was a constant visitor to the hall, often coming and going as he pleased. He was working on a novel about the hall before his death, so perhaps his spectre now lingers here, eternally contemplating his unfinished work.

A further shade at historic Athelhampton is that of the phantom cooper whose spectral hammerings have been reported emanating from the wine cellar next to

Below: *The State Bedroom is reputed to be the most ghostly bedroom at Athelhampton Hall and is haunted by a Grey Lady.*

Above: *Ghostly noises have emanated from the King's Ante-Chamber at Athelhampton Hall, despite the room being empty of all living things.*

Below: *The topiary gardens are haunted by a peaceful shade who is believed by some to be a clergyman who frequently visited the hall.*

the Great Hall. The barrels he is making are now long gone and no explanation can be found for the sound, which has been heard on numerous occasions. A head guide at the house heard an inexplicable sound during the day in the summer of 1998, but she described it as a loud banging noise, and certainly not the tapping that the legendary accounts describe.

Animal Magic

The most famous (or infamous) ghost at the hall is the phantom ape. The creature features in the Martyn family crest and in their motto, 'He who looks at Martyn's Ape, Martyn's Ape shall look at him'.

The story has it that the ape, which was actually a tame monkey, was the pet and companion of one of the Martyn daughters. Sadly, she was jilted in love and retired, distraught, to an upper room to drown her sorrows. The route she took led her through a secret passageway, possibly an early priest hole that was concealed in the walls of the house. Unnoticed by her, the pet followed. On reaching the top of the house she killed herself, unable to bear the reality of her situation. Unfortunately, the monkey had become locked in the secret passage and, unable to escape, it starved in its solitary prison. Even to this day its pitiful scratchings can be heard on quiet nights, clawing at the woodwork in a vain attempt to escape its ghostly prison.

Besides the well-known hauntings at Athelhampton there are other, lesser-known ghosts. The current owner's father experienced the ghost of a cat that once lived in the house. He heard it mewing on the staircase outside the Green Parlour and went to ask his son and daughter-in-law whether it had been fed that day. He was promptly informed that the cat had been runover the week before.

Above: *Dorset's ghostly Athelhampton Hall boasts of supernatural spirits both within the building and in the grounds.*

One of the house guides told me during a visit to the hall that two visitors had reported a strange occurrence in the Great Chamber. The rope barrier that hangs across the room to prevent visitors wearing down the ancient carpets was swinging violently back and forth despite there being no-one in the room.

The North Wing

The north wing of the house was built in the 20th century and is hired out as a private home. A couple who lived in the wing reported hearing loud banging during the night. Upon investigation there was no-one at their front door and there was no apparent explanation for the sounds.

Another tenant of this wing of the house recalled a guest at a barbecue saying he had seen the ghost of a maid walk through a wall. While a recent account tells of the sound of running footsteps in the King's Ante-Chamber, heard by someone in the Great Hall. When investigated there were no visitors in that area and the architecture of the house is such that it could not have been anyone else present in the house at that time.

A new spectre is the White Lady who has been seen walking through a gateway in the gardens. Who she is or why she has begun to haunt Athelhampton is unknown. There are other ghosts here, too: nameless wraiths that drift among the ancient trees and the darkened corridors, a man in Tudor costume and the phantom of Alfred Cart La Fontaine, who owned the property from 1891 until 1918. They all remain here in the place they once knew and loved.

Athelhampton stands proudly at the forefront of our haunted heritage, its decaying grandeur and restless spirits combining to create an atmosphere of otherworldliness which will enchant any ghost hunter or student of the psychic world.

CREECH HILL, BRUTON, SOMERSET

Above: *Creech Hill may look like just another West Country hill, but appearances can be deceptive, as this hill is haunted by a frightening elemental ghost.*

An early Roman-Celtic temple was discovered on the summit of Creech Hill, which dominates the landscape near Bruton in Somerset. The hill has had a reputation as being a place of ghosts and witches for many years, and in the 18th century two bodies of Norman-Saxon origin, which had been placed over each other in the shape of a cross, were dug up here.

A Blood-curdling Laugh

Local people recount tales of the hideous haunting that exists in the very bowels of the hill – a strange elemental ghost that rears up on dark nights, terrifying those who encounter it by chasing them out of the area while emitting a blood-curdling laugh.

One account tells of an unlucky farmer who came up against the phantom of Creech Hill. He found something lying in the road and when he approached it, it leered up at him and let out a chilling scream. He turned and ran as fast as his legs could carry him, but the 'thing' pursued him all the way home to his farmhouse. Upon arrival his wife glimpsed a 'black thing' retreating toward Creech Hill, laughing.

A second tale is that of another unfortunate percipient whose task gave him no option but to take a route across Creech Hill at night. He armed himself with a staff to defend himself and a lantern to guide his path, but no sooner had he reached the summit of the hill than a black mass erupted out of the earth, looming up before him as a 10-foot (3-metre) high phantom of repugnant appearance, screeching and laughing like a mad thing.

He struck out at it, but with no effect, as the staff went straight through his accursed tormentor. The poor man was subsequently rooted to the spot with fear until he was found later the following afternoon by two local farm workers and taken home. After several weeks convalescing from his terrifying ordeal he finally recovered, but was never quite the same man again. He spent his days peering through his bedroom window in the direction of the hill, almost as if something was beckoning him back to join it there, something nightmarish, something dark – the phantom of Creech Hill…

THE ANCIENT RAM INN, WOTTON-UNDER-EDGE, GLOUCESTERSHIRE

Tucked into the Gloucestershire countryside nestles The Ancient Ram Inn, a strange and quirky place built in 1189 and haunted by a number of ghosts. The inn is built on a ley line and sits atop an ancient site allegedly used for satanic practices. Evidence of such rites was unearthed when an archaeologist dug up the floor in the Men's Kitchen and discovered the bones of several children and two ceremonial daggers. Combined with other tales of murder and torment, this surprisingly picturesque building is a haven of supernatural activity and hundreds of visitors will attest to its paranormal heritage.

The Bishop's Room

The most haunted room in the dark, brooding building is the Bishop's Room – a bedroom on the first floor. When the building was a bed-and-breakfast establishment, many guests refused to sleep in the room and others fled in the middle of the night. Also, a ghostly monk haunts the area near an old priest hide in the Bishop's Room. Now, flocks of ghost hunters visit on a regular basis, many finding positive evidence of things they cannot explain.

The inn's ghosts are many and varied, and include a Roman centurion on horseback who startled a plumber by riding straight through a wall. This could be explained by the belief that the building is on the site of a Roman road.

Beyond the centurion, there is the cavalier, the shepherd, the old man who is seen from the outside sitting by a roaring fire in the Men's Kitchen – even though no-one is inside and no fire is alight – and an ostler called Tom who used to live in the hayloft and look after the horses when the inn was a coach stop. The inn is also haunted by the spectre of a young woman called Elizabeth who was murdered and buried in the foundations of the building. She is now known as the Blue Lady and wanders through the building carrying a lighted candle.

The Succubus

Most frightening of all, however, is the succubus that creeps into the beds of sleeping visitors. The current owner himself has experienced this phenomenon on many occasions.

Below: *Tales of satanic practices, ley lines and succubi surround The Ancient Ram Inn, hence its popularity with ghost hunters.*

TREASURE HOLT, GREAT CLACTON, ESSEX

Once known as Perles Farm, Treasure Holt stands today isolated among woods and meadows and can be accessed only by a small winding road. Parts of the building date back to 1138 and, although the precise history of the location is unclear, it is probable that the building was at one time an inn. Tales abound here of murder, witchcraft, ghosts and even hidden treasure.

Over the years the stories have changed and some may have been embellished, but there is no smoke without fire and a great many have reported seeing and feeling frightening things at Treasure Holt.

The Sin of Greed

Legend has it that a former innkeeper and his wife became so greedy that they encouraged wealthy travelling merchants to get drunk and then robbed them of their wares while they slept. If their victims woke during the looting the innkeeper would swiftly clobber them on the head and dump their bodies down the inn's well.

King Charles I (1600–1649) is said to have stayed at the inn on a rendezvous with a man named Simon who had been sent to pass on secret information. Following the meeting, Simon stayed at the inn where he was plied with drink. He soon found himself with a group of satanic revellers dancing wildly round a fire in the woods surrounding the inn. That night Simon sold his soul to the devil.

There is a ghost here, too, called Matthew, whose spirit can be seen hiding a box in the fireplace. There is a young woman in white who has been photographed in an upstairs window, and a robed figure was witnessed on the drive, while two cavaliers were spotted in the grounds.

Finally, a previous owner known as Uncle Percy has been seen looking in through the windows of the lounge.

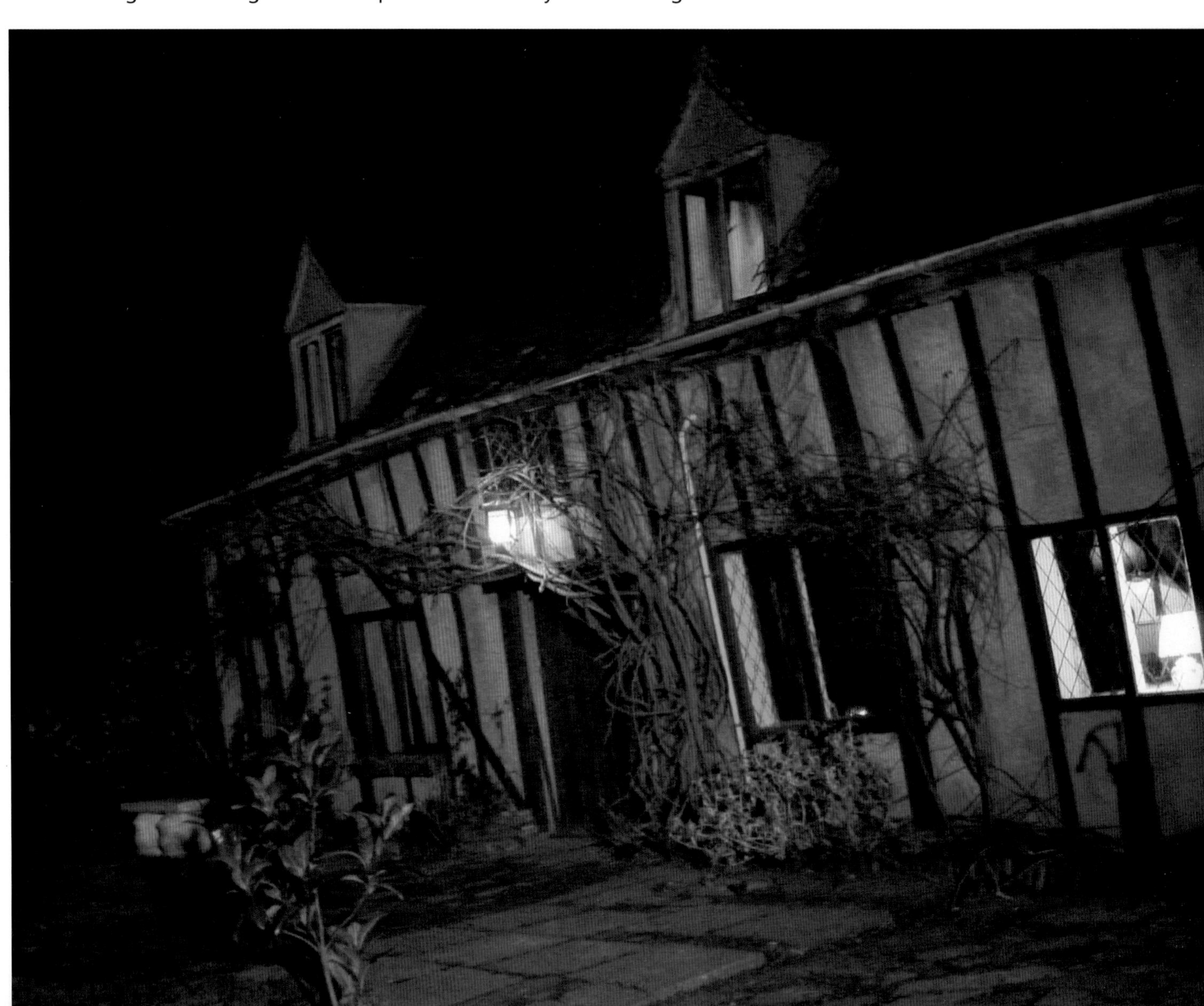

MUNCASTER CASTLE, CUMBRIA

Heralded as one of Britain's most haunted castles, Muncaster has been the subject of much paranormal investigation over many years. Researchers have recorded strange happenings here, including anomalous sounds and sightings of ghosts.

Tomfoolery

Many of the tales here revolve around Tom Fool, a former steward and jester, and from whom the term 'tomfoolery' derives. Although Tom is rarely seen at Muncaster, his dominant spirit continues to play tricks on people at the castle. Tom is said to have murdered a local carpenter who claimed to be the lover of Heloise Pennington – a daughter of the castle in the 16th century. The headless ghost of the carpenter is now said to wander the grounds and gardens of Muncaster seeking revenge on the fool and looking for his lost love.

Haunting activity frequently occurs in the Tapestry Room, where visitors have reported hearing footfall outside the bedchamber, seeing the door handle turn and the door open but there being no-one present – at least no-one visible. A child is often heard crying at the window of the bedroom and sometimes a ghostly lady is heard singing a gentle lullaby, as if comforting a child. The temperature in the Tapestry Room is also extremely unstable, and it has been known to plummet to icy depths in mere moments.

Other stories concern the White Lady who haunts the gardens and roadways around the castle. She is the restless spirit of Mary Bragg – a young girl who was murdered in the early 1800s on the road near the main gate.

Opposite: *Treasure Holt, now a rather benign tree nursery, has a long legacy of hauntings.*

Below: *Muncaster Castle in Cumbria is haunted by 'Tom Fool', who was a former jester and steward to the house.*

LLANCAIACH FAWR, TREHARRIS, MID GLAMORGAN, WALES

This grand, and haunted, Tudor manor house was built in the 1600s on the site of an earlier medieval settlement by Colonel Edward Prichard as his family home. It has the reputation of being one of the most haunted houses in Wales and, in the opinion of past residents and employees, the reputation is well deserved.

Seven Spectres

There are at least seven identifiable ghosts which make their presence felt in a variety of different ways, and probably several more whose identities are yet to be discovered. Strange sounds are heard frequently, including footfall in deserted rooms, laughter along passageways and voices on the stairs. The ghosts here are seen, felt or even smelt. In the past, instances have been recorded where the technical failure of equipment has been blamed on the supernatural presence in the building.

The ghost who travels most about the property is that of Martha, a previous housekeeper. Martha died suddenly and is, thus, now trapped in limbo. Although she has been sighted throughout the manor and spotted standing looking vacantly out of windows, there is one particular room at the top of the building which has become most closely associated with her ghost, and many visitors to the house have had strange encounters in this room.

One of the ghosts ventures beyond the walls of the house and, from his appearance, has been identified as a Victorian gentleman wearing a tall hat and a black cloak. He has been sighted inside the house, in the gardens, the meadow and even on the road near the manor.

Colonel Prichard

The most famous ghost at Llancaiach Fawr, however, is that of Colonel Prichard himself. He is seen and heard mainly in The Great Hall and the chamber that used to be his study. Staff at the house report that he is an anti-social ghost as he seems to take a dislike to visitors in 'his' house.

On the Grand Staircase the spirits of several children have been witnessed. On occasion they have been known to also haunt the corridor on the top floor. Another staircase at the back of the Cross Passageway is the haunt of the ghost of a limping manservant.

Many staff have had first-hand encounters of the ghosts in the manor and are happy to tell visitors about their encounters with the unknown. The manor also offers Ghost Tours at night for any particularly brave souls to endure!

Opposite: *The ghost of a headless carpenter is said to walk in the grounds of Muncaster Castle.*

Below: *The ghost of Colonel Prichard is prevalent at the manor house of Llancaiach Fawr.*

HERMITAGE CASTLE, LIDDESDALE, SCOTLAND

Remote and lifeless, the soulless shell of Hermitage Castle stands steadfast in the valley of Hermitage Water, inhabited only by the ghosts of those that have gone before. It takes a brave soul to visit the castle ruins alone and I have done so on a bleak November day and witnessed something of the castle's supernatural power.

The Spirit of De Soulis

The castle was erected in the 13th century and its name derives from a man known as Brother William who lived in this forsaken spot in the 12th century as a hermit – his cell may still be seen close to the castle.

The first stronghold was put up by the Dacre family and ownership later passed to the Comyns and subsequently to the De Soulis family. One particular member of the De Soulis family, despite being its lord for only a short time, established a reputation for being a wicked and evil man who savaged local beauties, murdered children and practised the black arts in the castle. History records show that he died as a prisoner at Dumbarton, but local belief has it that his local tenants turned against him and killed him by throwing him into a cauldron of boiling lead.

Either way, his spirit remains here, along with that of a fanged demon known as 'Robin Redcap' – his repulsive familiar sent to aid his nefarious deeds by the devil himself. Robin Redcap promised Lord De Soulis that he would never be bound by steel or rope in return for a constant supply of children's blood, and the Devil is said to have given De Soulis the power to summon him by banging three times on an old iron chest.

Other ghostly tales tell of a giant with magical armour and of a lady in white whose silhouetted figure can sometimes be seen atop the castle battlements in a flowing white dress – it has been suggested that she is the

spirit of Mary Queen Of Scots (1542–87) who visited the castle.

Former ITN Newscaster **Sandy Gall** had a ghostly encounter while filming at Braemar Castle in Scotland. Upon reaching a top-floor chamber he was engulfed by a feeling of a supernatural presence, so much so that the hairs on the back of his neck stood on end! He later discovered that the room had a reputation for being haunted by the sound of armed men fighting an invisible battle.

Someone at the Door?

When I visited Hermitage Castle I was surprised by its foreboding atmosphere and barren location. There was no curator at the gate, so I decided to take a walk around the grounds, as I reached the surprisingly small front door of the castle I turned to take in the vista. As I stood there, silent, on that bleak cold day a thunderous 'bang, bang, bang' came from the door behind me. I spun round but there was nothing to be seen. Upon investigation I found that the door had a large door knocker on it and surmised this must have been the cause of the sound – but there was no-one around and the wind was nowhere near strong enough to cause the knocker to bang.

I fled Hermitage castle swiftly and have since wondered on the cause of the sound I heard. Was it merely the wind banging the door knocker or was it wicked Lord De Soulis banging on his iron chest to summon the devil?

Opposite above: *It has been suggested that the ghost of Mary, Queen of Scots (1542–87) may be the phantom glimpsed atop the battlements of Hermitage Castle.*

Opposite: *Desolate Hermitage Castle has a reputation for evil hauntings.*

Right: *I personally witnessed a strange occurence at Hermitage Castle, which left me feeling seriously spooked!*

LEAP CASTLE, ROSCREA, CO. OFFALY, IRELAND

The remains of Leap Castle cast a sinister and frightening shadow over the Irish landscape. With some 20 different spectres in residence, Leap has acquired the reputation of being the most haunted castle in Ireland. Once the seat of the powerful O'Carroll family, it is now a mere shadow of its former self, having been all but destroyed by a terrible fire in 1922.

Below: *The fireplace in Leap Castle's Great Hall is visited by the ghost of an Elizabethan governess.*

An Educated Ghost

Local people avoid the castle at night, believing it to be a place of evil. It has been suggested by some researchers that the castle stands on a confluence of two black streams (negative ley lines) which constantly re-fuels the negative influences that inhabit the walls of the building.

The hauntings here include the spirit of a former Elizabethan governess, who was seen as recently as February 2002 by a visiting American tourist. The American lady had been left alone in the Great Hall by the rest of her party as she couldn't face ascending the spiral staircase to the upper rooms. As she waited, she supped some coffee by the fireplace. Suddenly, a tall harshly dressed woman in a black dress walked swiftly into the room, brushing the visitor as she went passed. The ghost proceeded to stir an 'invisible' pot on the fire before returning the way she came.

Another female haunting here is the spirit of a lustrous wild woman in a red gown. She dashes at witnesses, waving her arms around like a mad thing and wielding a large dagger. The ghost has been encountered in one of the bedrooms and her appearance is described as 'shining from within'. She is also said to leave a ghostly chill in the air after disappearing.

The owner of the castle has told me tales of other ghosts, too, including a 'harsh-faced' warder, a monk, an indelible bloodstain, an old man in black with a shiny bald head, a 'wild captain' who is seen wringing his skeletal hands in the castle grounds and a strange little man in green clothing described as having 'shiny things on his shoes'. This latter spectre sounds suspiciously like a leprechaun to me!

A First-Hand Account

When I stayed at the castle in 2002, one of my team saw the partial ghost of a small child on the first floor. The apparition was just of the child's head and neck and wore a white ruff round her neck. The spirit did not speak and melted into the walls when approached. The castle's owner has told me that this was the spirit of a child named Charlotte who is alleged to have died during a famine in the area. The ghost has been seen many times, particularly by the owner's 11-year-old daughter who seems to have an affinity with the spirit.

Reasons for the castle housing so many ghosts possibly include the fact that it was built on a site that was used by druids in pre-Christian times. And this may explain the presence of Leap's most frightening phantom – a gruesome, foul-smelling, part-human-part-beast spectre – which inhabits the castle's spiral staircase. This spirit is believed to be the embodiment of all the horrific and evil deeds that have taken place here. One sinister fact of note is that following the great fire in 1922 three cartloads of human bones were diiscovered in and removed from the oubliette – a chilling reminder of those who saw their last moments of life at Leap Castle.

Below: *The remains of Leap Castle, although still an occupied family home, are avoided by locals.*

Phantoms on Your Doorstep?

ARE YOU HAUNTED?

Talk to anyone you know and you will find a story of a haunted house in your neighbourhood – ghosts are a lot more common than most people think. But have you ever wondered if your own home is haunted?

Tell-Tale Signs of a Haunted House

- Do animals behave strangely in any area of the home? Cats and dogs are renowned for their ability to pick up on the presence of spectral residents.
- Have you heard unexplained noises? The most commonly reported sounds are knockings, raps, footsteps, voices, bells ringing or children crying. Sometimes these psychic echoes are attempts by the ghost to make contact. At other times they are just replays of things from the past.
- Do objects move around of their own accord? Some ghosts have a sense of humour and enjoy playing practical jokes. If you find your personal effects are being tampered with it is worth considering the possibility that it may be something other than a living person that is moving them around.
- Do you ever smell unusual or unexplained fragrances? It could be pleasant or nasty – sometimes the only manifestation a ghost makes is that of a spectral scent which lingers as a reminder of the person who lived there in the past.
- Is there a room that is always colder than the rest of the house despite being heated? Or is there a room or area that sends shivers down your spine every time you pass by? Look into the history of the home or site – you may discover that something sinister happened there long ago.
- Do you ever feel that you are not alone, even though there is no one else home?
- Have lights been seen in rooms that are unoccupied? If so, they may be occupied by a visitor from beyond!

HAUNTED HOMES FROM THE CASEBOOK OF THE GRFI

In these cases of haunted homes, some names have been replaced with pseudonyms to protect the owners' privacy.

HAUNTED HILL COTTAGE

West Wratting, Cambridgeshire

The following account was given by Rita – a previous owner of Hill Cottage.

'A few months after purchasing Hill Cottage my now ex-husband Charlie seemed to take on a different personality. Charlie became reckless, a spendthrift and a womanizer. He asked me for money when I had none, he bought new cars and wrote cheques that would not clear. Local villagers started to compare him to Dave, the deceased son of the previous owner of the cottage.

'One day, Charlie got a scare. He thought he saw me at the top of the stairs in a long dress, only to find me asleep in bed. Our dog would react strangely at 8pm each night – he would become agitated and sniff at the door to the study for about 10 minutes before settling again.

Above: *In haunted Hill Cottage the dog would regularly sniff at the study door in an agitated manner.*

'Other things happened, too. My four-year-old son woke one night to find a man with 'a horrible face' telling him to 'Keep quiet, there are children in here'.

'My own experiences began when I was moving a bed from upstairs down to the study. It got stuck on the staircase and I was going to go and ask for help to move it when, suddenly, it became much easier to manoeuvre, and using only one hand I guided it into place. I was later told this would have been impossible, as all the furniture that had previously been placed in that room was taken in through the windows. Also, while clearing out an inglenook fireplace one day, I was surprised to feel a hand on my back; this happened several times.

'Visitors who came to stay in the cottage often reported that during the night they had seen a figure standing in the spare bedroom staring at them. I avoided that room if possible, as it had a strange atmosphere that made me feel uncomfortable.

'The strangest thing, however, was the silver cigarette box – this would disappear from the coffee table every Tuesday, and reappear in the same place on Thursdays!

'After two years in Hill Cottage we were forced to leave as Charlie had not paid the mortgage for six months. I never did find out about the history of that haunted cottage, but I was glad to leave.'

THE HAUNTING OF MARLBERRY COTTAGE

Swanage, Dorset

Marlberry Cottage is a peaceful grey, stone house that nestles in what was the medieval hamlet of Swanage. Evidence dates the property from the 13th century and even suggests that parts of the building may date from even earlier, possibly from the Bronze Age. The cottage has been extended and remodelled time and time again, resulting in a house full of nooks and crannies. Dowsers have been able to locate a stream beneath the house, which runs beneath the sitting room and through the garden to the sea.

No country cottage should be without a ghost or two and Marlberry is no exception. The current owners have nicknamed their ghost Hester, after a former occupant whom they think may be the ghost. Hester seems to be active when alcohol is being served and consumed in the house, and on one occasion a bottle of wine drifted out of the wine rack, uncorked itself and proceeded to pour itself all over the owner!

On another occasion a guest was staying overnight in the lounge and awoke to witness a full apparition in the room, which proceeded to walk straight through a wall. This indicated to the owners that a door may have previously existed there. After chipping away the plaster, they uncovered a bricked up doorway in the exact spot where the ghost had been seen walking away.

THE MISCHIEVOUS SPOOK

Napton, Warwickshire

The sprightly spirit of a child from the mid-17th century is thought to be responsible for the mischievous goings on at a 600-year-old cottage in Napton. The first activity witnessed by the owners, Gill and Les, involved a pair of blue trousers that had been left over the back of a chair overnight. When Les came downstairs in the morning to put them on they had vanished.

During their time in the cottage, the couple have become accustomed to their resident spectre, whom they believe to be the phantom of Peter Sheasby – a 10-year-old boy who was due to inherit the cottage from his grandfather in the 1650s. Unfortunately, Peter died before his grandfather, which is why his spirit remains.

Gill and Les have never actually seen Peter, but his antics ensure that they are aware of him. On one occasion he moved a salt cellar onto a window cill and on another he hid a pair of scissors. The couple live happily with their ghost and even say goodnight to him – he is part of the family.

There is some evidence to back up the notion that the spirit is indeed that of Peter Sheasby. A young girl visiting a cottage near Gill and Les's went downstairs one afternoon and explained that she had been teased by a young boy. When questioned as to his appearance, the description she gave matched the clothing of children from the mid-17th century.

THE HAPPY GHOSTS OF KILBURTON HOUSE

Near Banbury, Oxfordshire

The following is taken from an account written by Mrs Edwards, who lived in Kilburton House for many years.

'Kilburton House is a 15th-century property that has a wonderful atmosphere. The ghosts there were calm and peaceful and I was never disturbed by them, merely haunted.

'The first ghost I sighted was that of a tall, elderly woman who was dressed in the fashion of the Edwardian era with a white blouse, black skirt and shawl round her shoulders. She had grey hair, which was set upon her head in a bun, and a look of serenity on her face. She looked at me and then disappeared; I have since identified her as the mother of one of the people that used to live in the house around 1909.

'The other spectral visitation happened while I was watching television one day. I was distracted by something and, as I turned, I was presented with a dark figure, which was either a hunchbacked man or a monk with a cowled face. The apparition seemed very short in stature, and I found out later that the floor level had been altered over the years, so he may have been standing on the previous floor level. He had a beautiful face and lovely features and I saw him so clearly that I could see the comb marks in his grey swept-back hair. He seemed to look beyond me and then disappeared. I only saw the ghosts during the first year I lived in Kilburton House; sometimes I wish I could see them again.'

THE GHOST IN THE BEDROOM

Bolton, Lancashire

The following is taken from an account by Sylvia who lives at Higher Farm.

'We bought our home in February 1994. At the time it was a derelict farmhouse with a collection of disused outbuildings amid 75 acres of farmland. We didn't move straight into the building, as it was in such a state that five months of renovation work was necessary to make it habitable. People had warned us that the building had a reputation for being haunted, but being local this didn't bother us and we took little notice of them.

'We had been told by a historian that the ghost of a cavalier was supposed to ride up the driveway to the farm and that there had been an earlier farmstead on the land before the current one.

'In 1644 there was a Civil War massacre in Bolton and the then owner of the farm – George Whowell – had been involved. Upon returning to the farm, he discovered that his wife and child had been victims of the massacre and he sought revenge upon the man who had slain his family. The farm went to ruin following the demise of George's family, but many years later the man responsible for the massacre was caught: it was the Earl of Derby. The earl was executed in Bolton town and the executioner who dealt the fatal blow was none other than George Whowell. George Whowell became a local hero and, after he died at a grand old age, his skull was kept for posterity in a nearby pub, where it still resides today.

'The events of this story all happened in the earlier farmhouse that stood on the site of our current home, so we were not bothered by it. All the same, we didn't tell Jack – the workman responsible for renovating the building – for fear that it might scare him away. We had hired a caravan for him to sleep in while working on the project and it was situated next to the farm building. Although the snow fell thickly that first winter in 1994, it was a warm and adequate base.

'During the first night on the job, Jack was unable to sleep and in the morning he explained to my husband that he had been kept awake for hours by the sound of horses outside the caravan. It had disturbed him so much that he had ventured outside to shoo them away, but upon opening the caravan door there was nothing to be seen and the noises instantly ceased.

'Puzzled by this, Jack examined the snow in the morning and to his amazement there were no hoof prints to be seen. After that first disturbed night, Jack reported hearing the horses many times. Often he described their sound as 'being on cobbles', which was most strange as there are no cobbles in the area – the house is basically in the middle of a field.

'We finally moved into the completed house in the summer of 1994. Soon afterwards, odd things began to occur. Two of my children said that during the night they had experienced the feeling of someone sitting on the bed; then my third child came downstairs screaming one morning that she had 'felt something sitting beside me' in her bedroom. That was the first time anything was experienced during daylight hours.

'My husband does not believe in the supernatural and has always maintained that the children had imagined their experiences, then, one day, he had an encounter himself. He was sitting downstairs when all of a sudden there was a lot of banging and noise coming from one of the upstairs rooms. He collected one of our dogs and ventured upstairs to confront the intruder, only to find there was no-one there and no windows open. The dog refused to enter the bedroom where the noises had been coming from.

'Over the years the experiences have died down, but we are still visited by 'something' sitting on the beds in certain bedrooms now and again.'

Above: *The skull of local hero George Whowell still resides in a local inn near to haunted Higher Farm.*

THE HAUNTED VICARAGE

Walton-on-Thames, Surrey

The following is taken from an account by local historian, Irene Sandells.

'There was once a haunted vicarage in Walton-on-Thames. Sadly, it is long gone, but the stories of its hauntings remain firm in the minds of those who witnessed them.

'The vicarage had several ghosts at one time, and in the late Victorian era the building was exorcised by the vicar, which seemed to extinguish several of the spectres. But one stubborn spirit stood its ground – the ghost of Old Sarah, a Cromwellian nurse, who was described by those who saw her as a large woman dressed in grey with a cap upon her head and carrying a bunch of keys. She had a habit of walking through walls where doorways had once been and even disturbed a curate who had a darkroom in the building where he developed his own photographs. While working in the darkroom one day, he suddenly witnessed a bright flash of otherworldly light from which the ghost of Old Sarah emerged. The light had originated from an area of the wall where a previous door had been and it wrecked his negatives – they all had a white streak on them!

'Another story relates to a woman named Harriet who worked in the vicarage in 1915.

'While the vicar was away on business it was the duty of the then curate, a Mr Riley, to stay at the vicarage to keep everything in order in his absence. Harriet had thought that Mr Riley had slept in the vicarage on the first night, as was arranged, even though she had not seen him arrive. She was surprised to learn from him the following day that he had fled the building in the dead of night as he had seen the ghost of a monk walk through his bedroom and vanish into the opposite wall. Sometime later, a panel was removed from the wall where the figure had disappeared and an old picture was discovered portraying a monk.'

A CHANNEL ISLES GHOST

St Peter Port, Guernsey

The following is taken from a letter I received from the owner of Ramee House.

'For the past 10 years, we have lived in a haunted house that was built in 1750, and we have experienced much supernatural activity. The previous owners told us that there was a friendly ghost attached to the building; she is a 12-year-old girl who is alleged to have drowned in a stream which used to run round the grounds of the house. The ghost of the girl was seen several times by the previous owners' daughter.

'The house is situated where ley lines are known to run, and this may be why we experience great surges of electrical activity which cannot logically be explained.

'When we first moved in to the house, we experienced a beautiful scent of strong perfume in certain rooms, but over the years the phenomenon has lessened and we now only experience this on rare occasions.

'Cold spots have been felt in a spare bedroom even during the warm summer months, and one night our daughter left her clothes on the floor of her bedroom and awoke the next morning to find them neatly folded on a chair!

'I have seen ornaments jump, not fall, from the top of the television to the floor, and objects from the mantelpiece or pictures from the walls are often found in the middle of the floor – always unbroken, just as if they have been placed there by someone, or something.

'The most puzzling phenomenon we have witnessed is when items go missing and then reappear months later exactly where we last left them. This has happened with jewellery and, most strangely, with a TV remote control, which disappeared during the renovation of a room that was completely stripped and redesigned. The remote control reappeared over a year later under my husband's shirt, which was lying on the new carpet in the room!'

WHISKEY-DRINKING SILAS

Bloxham, Oxfordshire

The following is taken from an anonymous account given to me in 1994.

'We moved to Ivydene in June 1924. It was a very hot summer and we soon discovered that we were living with a ghost. There were footsteps in the night and at times there was a strange atmosphere on the landing. Before we moved into Ivydene we would visit it every evening as it was only a few streets away. We used to take a few small articles with us each time, such as books, small pictures, etc. There was already a horse-hair chair in the cottage when we bought it. It was large, black, uncomfortable and cold to the touch. One evening, I cannot remember why, I stayed behind. When I was ready to leave I could not open the front door, I remember going and sitting in the horse-hair chair; there seemed to be a strange feeling enveloping the room, a feeling of resentment, and I was terrified. Luckily, my mother came to find me and she was surprised to discover me just sitting there in the chair. I did not mention my experience to her as I could not understand what it was that had frightened me, I only knew I was very pleased to see her.

'In 1925 there was a ghost that came in the daylight hours, although it was not actually seen. I was with my parents in the dining room and it was during the evening – about 9.30pm. There were five in our family: my parents, my two sisters, Elizabeth and Mary, and me; on this occasion Elizabeth and Mary were not in the house. To make it clear, I will describe the layout of the house: it was a double-fronted house with two bay windows with the front door opening into a straight hall. The hall led to a large conservatory and there was a kitchen at the back which had a large door leading to the gateway, from where there were double doors leading to the street.

'On this particular summer evening we all heard the double doors open and close and then the kitchen door open. We then heard footsteps, which stopped dead in the passage where we would hang our coats. The footsteps then passed along the hall and upstairs into my parents' bedroom, where they again stopped. My mother looked up from her writing and said, 'Go and see what Mary is doing in my bedroom.' Mary had been to play tennis at the local tennis club and it was the time of night that we expected her to return. I opened the door and went into the passage and paused because her coat was not hanging on the coat pegs. I went back into the dining room and told my mother. My mother then asked my father to go and see who was upstairs. He had not heard the footsteps as he was partially deaf and had been engrossed in a book. As he went up the staircase we went out into the garden to look at the upstairs window of my parents' bedroom from below. We soon saw my father's face at the window telling us there was no-one there. As we were standing, puzzled, in the garden my two sisters returned home and we explained what had happened. We then set about the house trying to find an explanation for the footsteps, but could find none.

'After this first encounter I was always slightly uncomfortable living at Ivydene. I often felt that something was physically trying to 'restrain' me while I walked along the landing and I never left my bedroom after nightfall. As time passed, my father, too, experienced something of the supernatural in our family home. On several occasions he told me that he had heard footsteps coming up the stairs and entering his bedroom before stopping at the side of the bed. He had a pull switch installed so that he could quickly turn on the light when the sounds occurred, but he never saw anything. My Aunt Kate also once witnessed the ghostly footsteps when the house was empty; she said it really gave her the creeps and made all the hairs on her arm stand on end.

'There was a tale that a young husband had had an accident in the yard and was taken to the bedroom now used by my parents to recover, but he died there before the severity of his condition was realised. We used to think that it was his spirit roaming around our home; his name was Silas. Whenever we heard a bump or a strange noise we used to say, 'Not to worry, it's only Silas'. My father used to joke that he had hidden a bottle of whiskey in life and was still trying to find it in death – but he never led us to it!

Above: *Was the ghostly presence in Bloxham searching for his hidden whiskey as one owner used to joke?*

'On the eve of my father's funeral in 1951, I was in the sitting room with my then husband, Arthur, and we both heard a pistol shot in the haunted bedroom. Even Arthur, who was stone deaf, jumped to his feet. Arthur went up to the bedroom to investigate, while I remained at the bottom of the stairs keeping an open retreat, but, as usual, there was nothing to be seen. In June that same year I had been out shopping in Banbury and when I returned I entered the house by the double doors that lead to the kitchen. As I opened the kitchen door I was shocked to see my father standing there in his usual clothes! As I quickly went towards him he turned and vanished along the passage. I followed, but knew he would not be there for he had been dead for some months. I was not afraid to see him, but I do think the rest of my family thought I had lost my senses when I told them.

'In June 1952 we moved away from Ivydene and I wasn't sad to leave. I had always thought that the house had somehow resented my presence, as if it had a personality of its own.

So ghosts don't just frequent crumbling castles and grand stately homes, they co-exist with the living in houses and streets. Perhaps there is a ghost down your road? Or perhaps you have one in your own home? Whether you live with the dead or you spend your time seeking them, they are, for the most part, harmless – simply a reminder of the past that in some cases becomes a rightful member of the household.

Fractures in Time

TIMESLIPS – AN ENIGMA FOR PARANORMAL SCIENCE

Timeslips are, by definition, a 'slip' in time whereby the paranormal influences that make themselves known in our world seem to be able to manipulate time itself so that we see and experience landscapes, environments, people and even architecture as it was in the past, or as it will be in the future. Tales of these kinds of experiences can be found in all countries, in all times.

THE WARDROBE TO THE PAST
Galmpton, Devon

The following is taken from a first-hand account:

'I had been looking after a senile lady for about three months before she passed away. She had become unpleasant towards her family and turned against them, as so often happens when senility creeps in.

'After she passed away, her husband carried on as if nothing had changed. He would talk to her all the time, as if she was just round the corner. He would tell her where he was going and say, 'Its alright, it's only me', as he came back in. He also kept a permanent shrine to her with photographs and flowers, which he expected everyone to talk to. I used to say, 'Hello Doris', as I came in, which made me feel pretty stupid but it kept him happy.

'One day, out of the blue, he was rushed into hospital as an emergency case and I went to visit him. He was very worried because he had left a briefcase with a lot of money in it at the bungalow where he lived. He did not trust his daughter for a variety of reasons, but the main one being that she was fond of her drink, and so he asked me to look for the briefcase and to keep it safe. The problem was that he could not remember where he had hidden it.

The Search
'A couple of days later I went to the bungalow with his daughter under the premise that I thought we should give it a good clean for when her father returned home. Luckily for me, she had been drinking and fell asleep in a chair. I searched the bungalow high and low, looking in all the drawers and cupboards, to find the briefcase.

I finally got to the father's bedroom, where a large old oak wardrobe stood dominating the room. I opened the door and saw that the wardrobe was still full of Doris's clothes, which surprised me as she had been dead for some time. Then, suddenly, there was this terrible feeling, as if something was surrounding my whole body in some sort of embrace. I couldn't breathe for several seconds and was completely drained. This experience quickly subsided and I collapsed onto the edge of the bed nearby. I looked up and the wardrobe was empty, except for a shoe box at the bottom. I could hardly believe my eyes – all the clothes that had been there moments before were gone!

'After taking a moment to gather my thoughts I was drawn to the top of the wardrobe where a decorative wooden panel existed. I reached up and behind the panel and to my surprise there was the briefcase! I quickly took out the money and hid it in my handbag, so that the daughter could not steal it, and left as quickly as I could. I have no explanation for the experience and for the clothes that were there and then suddenly disappeared. It was as if I had been transported back in time by Doris to help me find the hidden money.'

Above: *In Galmpton Devon, a carer for the elderly was directed to a hidden suitcase by a supernatural force.*

A NIGHT IN THE PAST
Near Avignon, France

In 1979, Geoff and Pauline Simpson decided to take a late summer holiday with their friends Len and Cynthia Gisby. They decided on a Spanish destination and planned to drive to Spain via France, stopping overnight en route.

At the end of the the first day they left the main AutoRoute (motorway) at Montelimar North and followed a sign for a local motel. Unfortunately, it was fully booked and they were advised to try some of the hotels along one of the smaller, less busy roads towards Avignon.

Quaint Rural France?

Cynthia noticed that, once they got away from the motel and began to navigate the smaller country roads, everything became extremely quiet, and she recalls laughing at the quaint, old-fashioned posters advertising such things as a local circus. After a while, the road became nothing more than a cobbled track, by which time they had pretty much given up hope of finding a bed for the night.

Then they came across a long, barn-like building. Len parked the car and went inside to discover that it was actually a restaurant. He went up to the old-fashioned counter and asked the gentleman there if the restaurant had accommodation. It took some time to get him to understand Len's English, but eventually it turned out that they did have two vacant rooms.

The Two Types of Timeslip

- **Retrocognitive Timeslip**
Timeslips in which the percipients witness experiences from times past.

- **Precognitive Timeslip**
Timeslips in which the percipients witness experiences from the future.

Above: *Two ghostly gendarmes featured in an immersion timeslip experienced by four holiday-makers near Avignon in France in 1979.*

Pauline remembers that the bedroom she entered was 'weird' – it had starched sheets, a thick furry bed-cover and no electricity. The window had no glass in it, just shutters, and there were no pillows, just a bolster across the top of the bed. The bathroom, too, was strange: it was reached by going down a long corridor and had a sunken bath and a spike on the wall on which the soap was stuck.

Actress **June Brown**, better known as *EastEnders* character Dot Cotton, has a psychic gift. She has witnessed premonitions throughout her life and has encountered numerous ghosts. While living in a Kent farmhouse she was haunted by a woman called Alice who had died falling down the stairs. June also witnessed a timeslip ghost in a disused railway tunnel with her friend Stephanie in Stratford-Upon-Avon. The pair had an uncanny feeling that they should not enter the tunnel and upon returning the next day it had completely vanished!

Increasing Peculiarities

Cynthia felt equally odd downstairs in the dining room, where a woman in an old-fashioned cap and dress was trying to ascertain what they wanted to eat. They were having language difficulties and could not explain their wishes, so in the end the ladies ended up with egg and sautéed potatoes and the gentlemen with steaks. The cutlery was also peculiarly heavy and basic in appearance.

All in all, the evening was decidedly strange, but following their hearty meal and local ales they laughed about how rural France was and about their adventure. They all retired to their bedrooms soon after dinner and slept soundly. Len remembers hearing only the sound of a distant train during the night – the road outside the hotel being strangely silent.

The following morning the group decided to take some photographs to commemorate their night's stay in this peculiar place. After Len and Geoff had snapped a few frames with their respective cameras they sat down to breakfast. The food was once again odd in taste and appearance. 'The bread was very heavy and coarse,' Cynthia recalls. 'It was sort of brown, like in wartime, and very sweet.' The coffee, too, was strange, and described by the group as 'black and thick'.

Their breakfast was interrupted by the entry of two gendarmes (policemen) wearing dark blue uniforms with gaiters up to their knees. This seemed odd because the group had seen gendarmes the day before dressed entirely differently to these two characters. They put it down to the 'old-fashioned charm' of the place and thought no more about it.

The next player to enter this peculiar scene was a young woman wearing a long purple dress and strange boots. She could have 'stepped out of a fancy-dress party', recalls Cynthia – but at 7am in this part of rural France that seemed very unlikely. Len decided to ask if there was a quicker way of returning to the main AutoRoute than the one they had taken to get there. He is convinced that, despite the language barrier, they had never heard of an 'AutoRoute', and he left them slightly bemused before packing their luggage into the car and asking the innkeeper for their bill. Minutes later he rejoined the group with a wide grin on his face. 'It was 19 francs!' he proclaimed. 'What, for the breakfast?' asked Geoff. 'No. For everything!' Len replied. The complete charge for two rooms bed-and-breakfast for four people with dinner and drinks came to the equivalent of £2.50.

The Return Journey

Following a fantastic sunny holiday in Spain the holiday-makers decided they would spend another night in the 'theme' hotel. So, they made their way off the same autoroute exit on their return journey. They found the big Montelimar motel where they had been advised to take the road to Avignon. After driving up and down the road four times they were dismayed and somewhat perplexed that they could not find the hotel. After making a thorough search of the area they came to the conclusion that the hotel simply wasn't there.

They are certain they were on the same road, for there were no other roads that led to Avignon from the autoroute. They even located the old-fashioned posters that they had found so amusing two weeks earlier and the lay-by where the hotel had been – but the hotel had simply gone. 'What struck us was that the trees down the road had been small during our first visit, and now they were huge.'

They put their experience down to tiredness and the heat and cast it to the back of their minds, but then on receiving their developed photographs from the holiday both couples were amazed to find that the photographs they had each taken at the hotel had not come out. There was no sign of them on the negatives either – it was as if they had never been taken.

Public Interest

In the early 1980s, this story was publicized by a local newspaper journalist and it received wide media attention. Several noted researchers became involved with the case and some intriguing questions were put to those involved, such as why did the innkeeper accept the modern money that Len had paid him? Why was there no comment on the group's clothing and their car? An answer seems clear to me. Rather than a slip back in time, timeslips are an entire immersive experience in which the paranormal entities in control of it are 'playing' with those involved. It may seem a far-fetched idea, but surely the very idea that we can go back or forward in time is equally far-fetched?

Further research into the case revealed some interesting facts. The dress worn by the woman in purple and the outfits worn by the gendarmes both matched the same time period – the turn of the 20th century. In fact, a French friend of Len and Cynthia told them that the gendarmes outfits they described had not been used since 1905. Bizarrely, when checking the price of accommodation and meals during the early 1900s in that region of France, travel agents Thomas Cook said that the cost for four people with dinner would have been about 19 francs. More local research

Above: *Despite being purchased in the late 1980s, David's envelopes hadn't been manufactured since the late 19th century.*

into the area showed that there was a building on the spot where the 'hotel' had been, long in the past. Locals couldn't remember if it had ever been a guest house, but they did inform the group that there had a been a local village police station next door – all at about the turn of the 20th century.

THE ENVELOPE SHOP

Norwich, Norfolk

In the late 1980s, 'David' was staying in Norwich. He didn't know the city as he had never visited before. His passion in life was stamp collecting, and he had been searching for some time for a shop where he could buy some small envelopes in which to store his spare stamps.

A Shilling Per Pack

David decided to try and find such a shop in Norwich. After some time pounding the local streets, he ventured down a small cobbled back street where he

Right: *At the turn of the 20th century, two spinsters experienced an amazing timeslip in the grounds of the French royal palace of Versailles, outside Paris.*

found a shop that had exactly what he was looking for in the window. David entered the shop and was served by a young girl wearing a long dress who told him that the envelopes were one shilling per pack. The price struck him as being very cheap, but far from complaining he gave her a 5-pence piece and left with his purchase. He couldn't understand why she had looked at the coin so strangely before putting it into the till.

He returned to his hotel after a pleasant day meandering the back streets of the ancient town, and the following day he decided to return to the shop to purchase some more envelopes as they were so ridiculously cheap. To his surprise, when he turned down the cobbled alley, the shop was not there. He retraced his movements from the previous day and found himself in the correct alley – but there was no shop. Confused, he found another stationery shop and showed them the envelopes he had bought. They had never heard of the shop he described and he was informed that envelopes of that style had not been produced since Victorian times.

THE PALACE IN THE PAST
Versailles, France

It was a hot summer's day in 1901 when two English spinsters, Miss Anne Moberley and Miss Eleanor Jourdain decided to visit the Palace of Versailles just outside Paris in France. They were distinguished ladies, one a principal of St Hugh's College, Oxford, the other the head mistress of an all-girls' school in Watford.

While casually exploring the gardens, they came across a fantastic phenomenon that has become the most quoted case of its type in the world. The full account of their experience is told in *An Adventure* – the book they published following their peculiar encounter with a timeslip.

The Adventure

Making their way towards the Le Petit Trianon area of the grounds, the first thing that was out of the ordinary to be witnessed was a woman shaking a white cloth out of a window, although this was only seen by Miss Moberley. This was soon followed by the sight of two gardeners with a wheelbarrow and spade. It struck the two friends that their attire seemed odd: long coats and tricorn hats. It was then that a feeling of great oppression, peculiarity and 'being withdrawn from the environment' overcame the ladies. They described

middle-aged woman wearing a pale low-cut dress. The woman was seated and was sketching. Miss Moberley remember that she had a mass of hair piled high upon her head, topped with a large hat. It later transpired that Miss Jourdain had seen the house, but only Miss Moberley had seen the woman. The ladies made their way along a terrace and met with a young gentleman who offered to show them around. As he spoke, the feeling of strangeness quickly faded and then he was gone.

Accounts Exchanged

Following their odd experiences, the ladies exchanged notes on what they had felt, seen and heard. They were at a loss to understand how one of them had seen certain people and things while the other had witnessed a different version of the same place. After writing full accounts of what each had seen and comparing them, it struck them that they had encountered something supernatural and something quite unknown to either of them.

This account has been subjected to much scrutiny over the years and it has been re-investigated by many ghost hunters. Many believe the ladies witnessed one of the most exciting timeslips ever recorded, but others say it was a fanciful romanticism of a day in the palace gardens. One interesting fact is that the description of the clothing and the buildings all made historical sense, and the description of the lady sketching matches that of Marie Antoinette herself.

the feeling as if they had somehow become separated from their surroundings and that the whole environment had become two-dimensional in some way.

Next, they saw a bandstand and a seated figure wearing a dark cloak and a sombrero. They had only taken this in for a minute when they heard the sound of footsteps approaching them from behind. They turned round to meet their new companion but there was nobody there. On turning round again they were met by a 'tall gentleman with dark eyes and curling black hair', who directed them with an excited smile towards the house.

No sooner had he disappeared from view than Miss Moberley was confronted with the spectacle of a solidly-built house in front of which was sitting a

THE VILLAGE TIME FORGOT

Bampton, Devon

It was a warm summer evening in 1993 when Alf and Eileen Roberts were driving back to their hotel in Dunster. They were holidaying in the West Country and became lost trying to navigate the winding lanes and roads of the area. They found themselves in a village

Above: *The peaceful Devonshire village of Bampton was the scene of a timeslip encounter in 1993.*

they didn't recognize and pulled over to consult their map. They noticed that the village was bright with the colour of flowers in hanging baskets, tubs and flowerbeds, and across the road from where they had parked they could see a small village green ablaze with flowers and a large wooden sign declaring 'Best Kept Village 1976 – Bampton'. After a short while they found their way out of the village down a road that was covered with a dense arbour of trees – it was so dark that Alf had to switch the headlights on temporarily.

Eventually, they made it back to the hotel for the night and the following morning they decided to return to the village to take some photographs of the beautiful flowers. They had no trouble getting back to Bampton, but when they arrived they had a surprise – all the flowers they had seen the day before had gone and the village green, far from being ablaze with colour, was just a patch of grass, with no sign. Confused, they drove around the rest of the village, but they failed to find any of the hanging baskets and tubs that had previously adorned each road.

Time Stood Still

After their initial disappointment and shock, two other peculiar happenings came to light. Alf recalls that as they entered the village the first time he had checked the time on his watch, it was 7.30pm and that on leaving the village he checked the time again, both on his watch and on the car dashboard, to find it was still 7.30pm. It was as if they had never been into the village at all. The couple also remembered that when they parked their car to consult the map Eileen had dropped a lit cigarette onto the page with Bampton on it. The cigarette had set the page on fire and had filled the car with smoke. On checking the page the following day there was no mark – not even a singe.

So did they visit a village from the past? Or were they simply lost and not where they thought they were? Whether you believe the story or not, upon checking historical records it was found that Bampton was the site of an early Celtic settlement that developed into a Saxon village of some importance, and Bampton was, indeed, the best-kept village in that area in 1976.

THE HAUNTED ARMOUR

The Bear Hotel, Woodstock, Oxfordshire

When I first began investigating ghosts and hauntings one of my first field trips was to The Bear Hotel, a 13th-century coaching inn which sits in the shadow of Blenheim Palace. There are tales of ghosts here, as you would expect, and that was my reason for visiting. However, while there I was fortunate enough to pick up a first-hand account of a timeslip from Brian, who was working as a general handyman at the hotel.

'It was during the day it happened, not in the dead of night as you hear these things usually take place.' Brian was a down-to-earth, middle-England character, and not a man prone to flights of fancy, nor one who would believe in anything supernatural. 'I was cleaning the armour breastplate that hangs over the fireplace in the dining room. It's a big piece of armour and takes some time to clean, so I was taking my time to ensure I did it justice. As I looked up from my work I was astonished to see that the whole room had changed. The furniture had gone and the fire was lit – it hadn't been a moment ago – and the whole room had a surreal peculiarity about it. It's hard to explain exactly, but it felt wrong. My heart was pounding and just as I was really starting to panic it changed back to its usual appearance. I stopped cleaning the breastplate after that, in fact I won't ever touch it again.'

Above: *This antique armoured breastplate was the trigger for a timeslip at The Bear Hotel in Woodstock, Oxfordshire.*

A FROSTY WELCOME
Ilchester, Somerset

Stanbury Thompson first recounted this tale to members of The Ghost Club, and Peter Underwood featured it in his book *Ghosts & Phantoms of The West*.

After completing his university education, Stanbury Thompson decided he would treat himself to a few days' rest in the beautiful West Country. A kind taxi driver advised him of a farm that took guests for bed-and-breakfast and he agreed to be driven there. The farm in question was situated in the middle of nowhere, down a long remote lane that had bramble bushes growing on either side. The driver informed him that Bramble Farm was owned by a Mr and Mrs Frost; they weren't farming people, but were the son and daughter-in-law of the last farmer who had passed away. The farm had no livestock now, it was just a big house.

Upon arrival, Stanbury was delighted with the place, a big white and timber-framed building with gables. He strode down the path and rang the bell, which he heard echoing around the large old house. After a moment or two he heard footsteps, so he signalled to the taxi driver that all was well and that the Frosts were at home. The taxi sped off back up the lane and Stanbury prepared to meet whoever was about to open the door.

Cold Hands

Eventually, the door was slowly opened by a tall, gaunt man whose appearance startled Stanbury for a few seconds. The man in the doorway was extremely thin and pale, with sunken eyes and a grey complexion. Stanbury enquired as to the availability of a room for the night and the man, who he assumed to be Mr Frost, replied with a smile and offered his bony hand to Stanbury. As Stanbury's and Mr Frost's hands met, a peculiar sensation soared through Stanbury's entire body – it was as if he had received an electric shock. This was quickly followed by a feeling of intense weakness and tiredness, which came over him so suddenly he could not quite fathom what was happening.

Mr Frost gestured for Stanbury to enter the house, which he eagerly did as he needed a bed now more than before! He followed the strange character down a long dark hallway and through two further rooms, all panelled with dark oak wood and filled with a variety of antique guns, swords and other regalia. The light was dim and the whole house exuded a gloomy and dismal atmosphere.

Upon reaching the parlour, a feeling of intense fear gripped Stanbury – beads of sweat formed on his brow and the whole feeling of the room changed. 'It was as if something unearthly was happening, I could not put my finger on why I was feeling so strange. It just felt very, very wrong.' Mr Frost seemed to sense Stanbury's discomfort and beckoned him to sit down and relax, telling him, 'You will be comfortable here, we won't disturb you.' The 'we' confused Stanbury, for he had not seen or heard anyone else in the house. Mr Frost then offered to cook him something to eat, to which Stanbury readily agreed as a meal and a warm fire were exactly what he needed. He drew his chair up to the fire while his sombre host left the room to prepare his meal. He was awakened from a short nap by the door opening and the return of his host, who watched intently as he ate the eggs and bacon he had cooked for him.

The Invisible Hostess

Following dinner, Stanbury pulled out a book and commenced reading, while always aware that he was being surreptitiously watched by Mr Frost. All of a sudden the door opened and shut by itself, and this was quickly followed by a heavy thud, as if some invisible person had entered the room and sat on the chair opposite Stanbury. Aghast, Stanbury looked to his host, who merely smiled and offered the calming words, 'We won't disturb you in the least, none of us. We are very quiet, reserved and retiring here, my wife and our two pets.' Stanbury realized at this point that he was not alone with Mr Frost, which in some way pleased him. He put the episode with the door and the thud down to exhaustion and imagination.

An hour or two passed with the two characters sitting in silence in the parlour. Stanbury read his book and Mr Frost stared intently into the flames of the fire; the only sounds were the ticking of the grandfather clock and the occasional hiss or spitting of the fire. Stanbury began to wish he had chosen a livelier break for himself. Bramble Farm began to lose its initial charm and seemed dark, eerie and somewhat ghostly as the night set in.

Without any warning Mr Frost broke the silence. 'Peter, Peter', he said and bent down as if to stroke a cat, Stanbury then heard a loud purring and felt something brush heavily against his leg and move off, but he could see nothing. This was the last straw, if it hadn't been for the storm that had swept up outside and the rain lashing against the window panes he would have left there and then. But, with nowhere to go and no hope of leaving in this weather, he hurriedly made his apologies and, petrified, stood up to make a hasty exit to bed.

As if his terror could not escalate any further, what happened next made his eyes almost pop out of their sockets. Mr Frost called, 'Martha, pray go and see to the gentleman's bed', while looking at the empty chair from which the earlier thud had come. Next, footsteps made their way across the room and the door opened and closed itself, clearly showing that someone had left the room. Worse than that, Stanbury realized that whoever or whatever it was had obviously been sitting opposite him all night! It struck him at this point that the house was full of ghosts and that he was at their

mercy. As he considered his dilemma he once again became aware of footsteps entering the parlour, at which point he was informed by Mr Frost that his room was ready for occupation.

Invisible Pets

As he made his way towards the parlour door, barely able to walk due to the adrenaline rushing around his body, a further ghost appeared to enter the room. From the sound and the welcome given by Mr Frost, he realized this must be a dog, but one of a spectral and invisible nature. Stanbury practically ran out of the room and bounded up the staircase to a room that had some degree of light coming from it. He slammed the door shut and locked it by wedging a chair underneath the handle and hastily switched off the light. His mind was racing, making sleep impossible.

As he lay on the big oak bed, contemplating the experiences of the evening, he became aware of a deep purring. Swiping his hand out he felt it make contact with something furry and solid, which was followed by a thud hitting the floor. Immediately, he switched on the light and searched the room, only to

Left: *Author Stanbury Thompson spent a night filled with fear at Bramble Farm near Ilchester, the scene of an incredible timeslip.*

find that he was alone in the chamber, with no trace of anything either living or dead. Following the encounter he was intent on staying awake through the night, fearing what else may visit him during the twilight hours. Noises from the rooms below continued for some hours. Laughing and talking, a dog barking occasionally and the general sounds of a lived-in house echoed through the floor. Finally, exhaustion caught up with Stanbury Thompson and he fell into a deep sleep.

A Hasty Exit

The following morning Stanbury awoke with a start and dressed himself in the utmost haste. He was downstairs in minutes and attempted to locate Mr Frost to settle his bill, but he found the entire house deserted and deathly quiet. He left, almost running down the path to the garden gate. He was met by a sports car pulling up the lane from which two figures quickly emerged to enquire what he was doing there. Realizing they must in some way be connected to the lonely farmhouse he told them he had been a guest of Mr Frost the previous night and had endured an evening of phantoms and fear. Somewhat surprised, the young driver of the car asked Stanbury to elaborate and introduced himself as Mr Frost.

Stanbury told him his story of the gaunt man, the invisible cat and dog and the footsteps. He was then informed by the young Mr Frost that there was no one in the house. He and his wife had been away the last few nights and that the man he had described didn't exist, at least not any more. It would seem that the people he had encountered had been the ghosts of the parents of the younger Mr Frost. Stanbury learned that old Mr Frost and his wife had been fond of animals, in particular their pets: Lassie a sheepdog and Peter a tabby cat. They had all died in the farmhouse at various times in the past.

Following his experience, Stanbury enquired with friends who had knowledge of the psychic world and he was correctly informed that the reason he had seen only Mr Frost's spectre visually was because he had made physical contact with him through the handshake when they first met. This had given the ghost the energy to maintain its apparition and was also the reason for the sudden and inexplicable tiredness Stanbury had experienced. He always remembers his startling night in Somerset, a county he now avoids if at all possible.

Sleeping With Spirits

SPEND THE NIGHT WITH A GHOST – IF YOU DARE!

There is nothing quite as exciting as roaming around a creepy castle searching for spirits, but this is not everyone's idea of a good night out. For those of you who want to ghost hunt in style, why not book yourself into a haunted hotel – there are hundreds all over Britain and Ireland. Here, I have selected a few of the better ones for you to try. However, please be warned: a peaceful night cannot be guaranteed...

ENGLAND

Amberley Castle Hotel
Near Arundel, West Sussex
Tel: 01798 831992

Amberley Castle is haunted by a kitchen maid named Emily, who is seen in the Herstmonceux bedroom and in the vicinity of the kitchens and restaurant. The chef has even lovingly named a pudding after her!

How Emily met her maker is uncertain, as is the reason for her haunting. Speculation suggests that she died during childbirth or of malaria. It is, however, known that a certain Bishop Rede, who was responsible for building the castle's curtain wall, seduced young Emily on many occasions while the castle was owned by the church in the 14th century. She died soon after, and the real story may be that she killed herself and her baby by jumping off the 60-foot (20-metre) high battlements.

Bear of Rodborough Hotel
Stroud, Gloucestershire
Tel: 01453 878522

On misty winter nights a headless coachman is said to drive his ghostly coach and four horses along the road outside this hotel.

Left and opposite: *The Herstmonceux guest bedroom at Amberley Castle has associations with Emily, Amberley Castle's ghost. Emily is believed to have climbed the stone spiral staircase, which is accessed through the Herstmonceux room, to the battlements, from where she threw herself and her baby to their deaths.*

Above: *When I spent a night at Thetford's Bell Hotel, I was fortunate enough to encounter the ghost of innkeeper Betty Radcliffe.*

The Bell Hotel
King Street, Thetford, Norfolk
Tel: 01842 754455

There is a story of a phantom fisherman haunting the smoking room of the Bell Hotel, but Betty Radcliffe – a successful and affluent inn-keeper who owned the building in the 18th century – is the hotel's principal ghost.

After meeting a young ostler who was passing through the town she fell completely in love with him, but he shunned her approaches and so, with a broken heart, she jumped to her death from the balcony outside Room 12. Guests often report manifestations of her ghost in the room, and I have stayed there alone overnight and experienced something I cannot explain.

I awoke in the middle of the night and, amid the darkness, saw a misty shape in the form of a figure. Others have reported the sound of sobbing or interference with the furniture or the television in the room. I also detected a spectral scent that I could not explain during my stay. However, what intrigued me most were the handprints inside a glass-covered frieze which, although wiped clean every night, have always returned. I'm not sure if they were there when I went to bed, but they were certainly there in the morning...

Roger Moore encountered a frightening phantom while staying at The Angel Hotel in Surrey. For two consecutive nights his sleep was disturbed by a misty figure floating across the room towards him. On the third night he left a Bible on his bedside cabinet, open at Psalm 23. This seemed to scare away the spook in the room as Roger slept soundly until the following morning.

Bestwood Lodge Hotel
Arnold, Nottingham
Tel: 0115 920 3011

This Gothic pile was originally a royal hunting lodge and later became a rendezvous for King Charles II (1630–85) and his mistress, Nell Gwynn. Gwynn was an orange-seller before becoming an actress, the profession through which she met the king. Sometimes the scent of oranges wafts around the hotel without any logical explanation.

The sound of children crying and of disembodied voices has also been reported, along with sightings of ghosts in medieval apparel. So frightened was a chambermaid in the 1980s that she quit her job because of the ghosts. Most recently, in November 2002, a plant display was thrown across the public bar by an unseen presence.

The Broadway Hotel
The Green, Broadway, Worcestershire
Tel: 01386 852401

Dating back to the 1400s, this building, in one of the prettiest villages in the Cotswolds, was originally used

as an abbot's retreat. Now a luxurious country hotel, it boasts a White Lady ghost whose identity is unknown – a challenge for a medium, perhaps?

Above: *Bestwood Lodge Hotel in Nottinghamshire is haunted by the sweet-smelling spirit of Nell Gwynn (1650–87), as well as by a poltergeist.*

The Bull Hotel
Long Melford, Suffolk
Tel: 01787 378494

Erected in 1450, this building was the home of a wealthy wool merchant until 1580, when it became an inn.

Richard Evered was a 17th-century yeoman farmer who frequented the inn with his friend Roger Green. One fateful night in July 1648 an argument broke out between the pair and the brawl ended with Richard stabbing his friend to death; he fled the Bull, leaving Roger dead on the hall floor. Roger's body was laid out overnight in what is now the lounge, but when morning came all signs of the body had gone and it was never recovered.

Since 1648, reports of furniture moving and of doors slamming inexplicably have been made, so much so that the room above the lounge, which is the focus of the disturbances, was sealed off for a time and became known as 'the haunted room'.

Coombe Abbey Hotel
Binley, Coventry
Tel: 024 7645 0450

This former abbey is crawling with ghosts, the most famous being that of Abbot Geoffrey, who was murdered by one of his peers in 1345. His ghostly form has been sighted gliding from the cloisters area, and it is he who is blamed for throwing glasses around in the banqueting kitchens. There has been a confirmed ghost sighting in the last 10 years. It happened during a medieval banquet, and the lady who saw the abbot presumed him to be part of the fancy-dress celebrations – until he vanished into thin air.

Another ghost makes the sound of dainty footsteps on the old cobbled courtyard, while a third spectre is a green-eyed gypsy woman named Matilda who haunts the stable block. Over 300 years ago, once it had ceased to be a religious building, Matilda fell pregnant by the master of the house. After delivering a still-born

Above: *A good night's sleep is unlikely at The George & Pilgrims Hotel in Glastonbury, as the ancient building is home to an array of paranormal phenomena, including a phantom monk, strange lights and the inexplicable smell of cigar smoke.*

child she was spurned by her lover, so she laid a curse on his family, whereby each first-born male would only live a short life and die before his 30th birthday. It seems to have come true, with the most recent young heir passing away a few years ago.

Other ghost stories are connected with the roads around the abbey. There is a phantom horseman at the appropriately named Shiver Corner and a spectral woman on a bicycle.

The George Hotel
High Street, Colchester, Essex CO1 1TD
Tel: 01206 578494

Originally a private house dating back to 1494, The George is now a fine hotel which subtly blends the wonders of the past with the luxuries of the present.

Over the centuries the building has been remodelled and extended several times. The somewhat plain and understated exterior belies the complex layout of rooms that lies within and, like many ancient inns of England, The George has its own resident ghost.

Aptly named George, the ghost makes its presence known in several friendly ways. Ian Claydon, an employee at the hotel, told me that while on duty in the lounge over the Christmas period in 1999 he distinctly heard a voice call, 'Ian… Ian', but he could not explain who – or what – had made the noise as there was no-one else around at the time. Just days later he recalled hearing the sound of chitter-chatter or sibilant whispering emanating from the kitchen area. Upon immediate investigation, he found the kitchens were empty, in fact there was nobody else in the entire building.

The George & Pilgrims Hotel
1 High Street, Glastonbury, Somerset
Tel: 01458 831146

Built in 1475, this is one of the oldest buildings in Glastonbury, a town with strong associations with the paranormal.

The George & Pilgrims has a ghostly atmosphere downstairs and a haunted bedchamber upstairs. Spectral cigar smoke, a ghostly monk and blue lights have all been reported.

Jamaica Inn
Bolventor, Cornwall
Tel: 01566 86250

This famous inn stands in an isolated spot on Bodmin Moor and is haunted by several different ghosts. A man sitting on the wall outside the building has been reported many times since 1911. He is thought to have been a sailor who was lured from the pub, robbed and killed.

The psychic echo of a coach and horses pulling up has been heard on the cobbles in front of the inn. Inside, there is a man in a cloak and tri-cornered hat, and the sound of footsteps echoes along deserted corridors late at night.

The Lord Crewe Arms
Blanchland, County Durham
Tel: 01434 675251

Situated near the site of an ancient monastery and originally built as the local abbot's house, this quaint inn is home to one of England's northernmost ghosts, that of Dorothy Foster, a heroine of the 1715 Jacobite uprising. Dorothy's brother was part of the rebellion, and after being captured and taken to Newgate Prison in London, Dorothy followed him and aided his escape to safety in France. Her spirit now haunts the Bamburgh Room.

Lumley Castle Hotel
Chester-Le-Street, Durham
Tel: 0191 389 1111

Built by Sir Ralph Lumley in the 14th century, this grand castle is haunted by his wife, Lily. She is said to emerge from a well in the basement of the castle, where her body was cast after she was murdered by priests because she refused to follow the Catholic faith. Her spirit now drifts around the corridors and passageways in a permanent state of melancholy.

The Mermaid Inn
Mermaid Street, Rye, East Sussex
Tel: 01797 223065

This beautiful old building dates back to 1156 and has been described as one of England's most haunted inns. The ghosts are many and varied and include a pair of phantom duellists, complete with doublet and hose, fighting with rapiers in the Elizabethan chamber – Room 16. The victor is seen to throw the vanquished duellist's body down a secret staircase and the scene then fades away into the brickwork.

Other ghosts include an old-fashioned gentleman in Room 19; a white lady who pauses to peer at sleepers in Room 5 (she is a former chambermaid who was killed for discussing the exploits of a local smuggler); a grey lady who makes clothes wet in Room 1; a haunted rocking chair which moves of its own volition in Room 17 and a ghost in Room 10 that scared a bank manager and his wife so much that they left the room in the middle of the night and refused to return! There is also a 'cursed chair' in the Giant's Fireplace and an interesting 'witch ball' in the Mermaid Parlour.

Above: *Made famous by the novelist Daphne du Maurier, Jamaica Inn has ghosts that include a sailor and a man in a cloak and hat.*

Below: *The beautiful and historic Mermaid Inn in Rye, East Sussex is one of my favourite haunted hotels. Almost every room has a ghostly tale attached to it, and the bar sells an excellent selection of ales to help you through a haunted night.*

I have stayed here overnight on several occasions, witnessing a few minor inexplicable occurrences. However, while it remains one of my favourite haunted inns, I have yet to see an actual ghost here.

Prince Rupert Hotel
Butcher Row, Shrewsbury, Shropshire
Tel: 01743 499955

Room 6 is visited by the ghost of a young woman eternally seeking a husband; she was jilted on her wedding day and subsequently committed suicide.

Royal Castle Hotel
Dartmouth, Devon
Tel: 01803 833033

This beautiful hotel has a long, ghostly heritage. In the dead of night the sound of a horse-drawn carriage rumbles through a former courtyard, which is now part of the interior of the hotel. Be careful not to listen out for it, though, as it spells doom for all who hear it.

Other ghosts include a female figure, a haunting in Room 10 and a ghost that throws guests' clothes onto the floor in Room 22.

The most astounding tale dates from the mid-1990s, when two duelling spectres were seen fighting in the courtyard section. The night porter who saw this spectral spectacle said it was also raining inside the hotel while he witnessed the duel, and that some, but not all, of the furniture was wet! Four night porters in a row have handed in their notice because of the haunted nature of this hotel.

Below: *The Talbot Hotel in Oundle is haunted by Mary, Queen of Scots (1542–87), whose spirit was introduced to the building through a staircase.*

The Talbot Hotel
New Street, Oundle, Northamptonshire
Tel: 01832 273621

Frequent sightings are reported here of the ghost of Mary, Queen of Scots (1542–87). The reason behind the haunting is believed to be the hotel's staircase, which was transported in its entirety here from nearby Fotheringay Castle where Mary was imprisoned before her death. Her ghost has thus been introduced to the hotel through the staircase upon which she must have walked many times.

There is a second ghost here of a wailing or sobbing woman, who may have been one of Queen Mary's maids. On rare occasions this spirit (it is assumed to be the same wraith) is also reported to have been heard singing.

The Whately Hall Hotel
Horsefair, Banbury, Oxfordshire
Tel: 0870 4008104

Originally named The Three Tuns, the Whately Hall Hotel has been a leading hostelry for Banbury's most important visitors for centuries. The building was licensed in 1677, and is said to have been the inn where author Jonathan Swift (1667–1745) penned part of his epic novel *Gulliver's Travels*.

The hotel's principal ghost is Father Bernard – a 17th-century Catholic priest who met his demise in the building. On 6 September 1687, a group of local clergy, which included Father Bernard, were dining in what is now Room 52 – right at the top of the building. This was a secret meeting place for the priests who were forced into hiding because of the religious intolerances of the day. Upon the arrival of their persecutors, a bell alerted the priests that they should exit the building by the secret staircase that runs down through the walls of the building to the cellars, where they could then access a maze of escape tunnels beneath Banbury.

One Paul Heuston had been enjoying a drink that evening and decided to pull the bell chain in jest, thus frightening the priests into escaping. Unfortunately, for Father Bernard it was all too much, and he collapsed and died of terror. Since then, his spectral form has haunted the hotel, in particular Room 52. It has been seen hovering at the secret staircase entrance in a black smock. Maybe he is seeking the prankster Paul Heuston, who himself was later murdered by Father Bernard's incensed colleagues on discovery of the practical joke.

WALES

Castle Hotel
High Street, Conwy
Tel: 01492 582800

There were once two ghosts in this Georgian hotel. The first, now at peace, was of a chambermaid who requested that upon her death she be buried on the Isle of Anglesey. When she passed away, her wishes were ignored and she was laid to rest in the local churchyard behind the hotel. Her spirit sought revenge by making a nuisance of itself around the hotel until, eventually, her body was re-interred on Anglesey in accordance with her wishes.

The second spirit is still present. It is a boisterous poltergeist known as George. It fills ashtrays with water and generally makes a mess around the place, much to the amusement of the guests and to the annoyance of those who have to clear up after it!

Maesmawr Hall Hotel
Caersws, Powys
Tel: 01686 688255

This 16th-century Grade II listed timber-framed building is haunted by Robin Drwg – a phantom bull. It took seven clergymen to exorcise his spirit in years past, but today things of a paranormal nature are still being experienced.

Maes-y-Neuadd
Harlech, Gwynedd, Wales
Tel: 01766 780200

The poet Robert Graves (1895–1985) described this country property as the most haunted house he had ever been in. Here, ghosts appear in mirrors and a violent poltergeist haunts the building.

Outside in the grounds, the spectre of a phantom yellow dog has been seen, each time heralding a death in the house.

Ruthin Castle Hotel
Ruthin, Denbighshire
Tel: 01824 702664

Majestic Ruthin Castle is home to the spectre of a knight wearing just one gauntlet; a ghostly ball of glowing light, which is the most commonly reported sighting; and a lady in grey, who has met several of the castle's workers in recent years.

SCOTLAND

Culcreuch Castle Hotel
Fintry, Stirlingshire
Tel: 01360 860555

The Chinese Bird Room at Culcreuch Castle Hotel is an elegant bedchamber haunted by a white-clad shape and the sound of spectral bagpipes. Diners have also witnessed the strange music emanating from beneath the floor of the dining room.

Below: *The Chinese Bird Room at Culcreuch Castle Hotel is sometimes haunted by the sound of bagpipes.*

Above: *Kinnity Castle Hotel has several ghosts and a gloriously enchanting atmosphere, which almost transports you back in time.*

Left: *Ghosts abound at Kinnity Castle Hotel, and the Library makes a perfect Base Room from which to conduct investigations.*

IRELAND

Kinnity Castle Hotel

Birr, County Offaly
Tel: 00 353 509 37318

This is my favourite hotel in the world – its medieval charm and gloriously spooky atmosphere will please any ghost hunter. At night, the candlelit hallways take you back centuries and, if that's not enough, it has several hauntings, too.

The banqueting hall is home to a ghost in a cowled robe, seen only at night; a ghostly, shadowy shape was seen in the Geraldine Bedroom in March 2001; and a towel was moved and a door opened by a spook in the Hugh O'Neill Room during the same month.

AFTERWORD

I first met Jason in 2001. It was a chance meeting at a paranormal event to which we had both been invited. This event resulted in the pair of us becoming good friends. I find Jason a real breath of fresh air; his youthful enthusiasm for his careful research is an inspiration to me in my work. His energy is endless, and his willingness to research human potential in the field of the paranormal is tireless.

This wonderful book is invaluable. It is a source of factual information that is both helpful and interesting – a must for anyone, from the tentative beginner to the ardent seeker of ghosts.

I have learned a lot from its pages, and Jason's descriptions of the various spectres and their haunting grounds are unique, making it a who's who and what's where of ghosts that is easy to read and follow. I have witnessed my own fair share of wonderful phenomena the world over: from Tachee, a North American Indian Chief who spoke through me in his native tongue, to a small child named Rebecca, who revealed through me how she burnt to death in a St Albans' hotel and came to visit me again while I was in Cyprus.

It is my great wish that Jason and I continue our research into this most poignant of subjects and, ultimately, encourage you to open your mind and realize the huge potential that each of us have at our disposal. Hopefully, this book will help you in your ghost-hunting endeavours, so you, too, will experience a close encounter of the spiritual kind.

I would like to wish you every good fortune and, most of all, love, as I have found it to be the only thing that transcends the experience we call death.

Marion Goodfellow, Television Medium

Are You Brave Enough to Become a Ghost Hunter?

If you would like the opportunity to take part in professionally organized ghost-hunting events in the Britain you can become a member of the Ghost Research Foundation International (GRFI). For more details, visit the website at: www.grfi.org or write to:

GRFI
2 Garden Walk
Ashton Upon Ribble
Preston
Lancashire
PR2 1DP
United Kingdom

Britain's biggest annual ghost conference is held during Hallowe'en each year. To find out how you can take part, visit www.ghost-con.com for more information.

If you would like to meet the author, you can book tickets to a 'Scariest Places In Britain' event by visiting www.scariestplacesinbritain.com.

GLOSSARY

APPARITION
A Stage 4 manifestation that is sometimes, but not always, visible to the human eye.

BLACK STREAM
A ley line of negative influence. Black streams absorb and exude negative feelings and vibrations. They can induce illness, headaches and, more seriously, depression and degenerative diseases. Black streams can be reversed by the use of crystals and by some psychics and mediums. They attract negative entities and are often linked to the presence and creation of elemental ghosts.

CASPER EFFECT
The appearance of wispy, transparent or translucent Stage 1 ghosts on photographs or video film, so-called because of its similarity in appearance to the fictional ghost character 'Casper, the friendly ghost'.

CLAIRAUDIENT
A medium or psychic who receives information from the other side in the form of sounds.

CLAIRSENTIENT
A medium who receives information from the other side by experiencing feelings, including physical ones.

CLAIRVOYANT
A medium who receives information from the other side by 'feeling' information, and relays it in one's own words.

DEMATERIALIZATION
The dissipation of a materialization, i.e. when a ghost vanishes or disappears.

ECTOPLASM
A sub-physical substance that can sometimes be seen with the naked eye. The word originates from the Greek 'ektos' and 'plasma' meaning 'exteriorized substance'. The structure of a ghost is believed to be made up of ectoplasm, and it apparently takes form in our physical world by manipulating energies such as electricity and human energy. The more energy available, the more physically 'real' the ghost becomes, until it climaxes in a complete manifestation.

ELECTRONIC VOICE PHENOMENA (EVP)
A recording of voices of the dead, that occurs at a frequency not audible by the human ear.

ELEMENTAL GHOST
A non-human ghost form that exists on a lower level of existence than other ghost types. Elemental ghosts are an embodiment of the actions and intents that have taken place in the ghost's haunting ground. They have limited intelligence and are thought to be created by extreme positive or negative energy that is put into a location over a long period of time.

Elemental ghosts can be created by occult ritual; extremes of intent (good or evil) by humans in the location; actions, experiences and emotions that take place at the location, such as murder, torment, suffering, happiness, love, hate, etc.

Elemental ghosts of a positive orientation are often thought of as protectors or sentinels of buildings or locations. The presence of a positive elemental ghost can be beneficial to a place or person. Elementals of a negative orientation can cause negative effects in much the same way as black streams can.

ESP
Extra Sensory Perception is a power beyond the normal five senses.

ETHER
The fifth element thought to permeate all space. Ether is believed to be the only element conducive to ectoplasm formation.

The acceptance of the existence of ether could help explain why some psychic manifestations appear 'out of thin air' or in apparent levitation and not resting or standing on anything solid. These ghost manifestations are manipulating the ether as a source of stability.

EXORCISM
The ritual of dispersing a ghost from a location or person, usually against its will. Appointed exorcists of various faiths, especially Roman Catholic, normally conduct these rituals. It is a fact that, even today, every diocese in Britain has its own appointed exorcist, although the Church keeps this area of its work closely guarded.

GENIUS LOCI
The 'spirit' of a place. This can be affected by the people who live in the place; by ley-line orientation (positive or negative); by events that occur in the place, such as murder or extreme suffering; and by other inputs of positive or negative influence.

GHOST HIGHWAY
A term for a ley line that is used to explain how ghost entities travel from one place to another, in the same way that we use roads; also known as ghost paths.

GHOSTPRINT
A handprint left in flour or dust by a spectre.

GHOST RESCUE
The work of psychics or mediums who apparently release entities from the ghost realm and help them reach the afterworld. Similar to exorcism, except that techniques used in ghost rescue are far gentler, and some believe kinder, as ghost rescue takes into account the wishes and feelings of the ghost, whereas exorcism does not.

GHOSTSTEP
A footprint left in flour or dust by a spectre.

JINX FACTOR
Locations subject to the 'jinx factor' bring about camera malfunctions, video equipment jamming or inexplicable interference by supernatural agencies to reclaim photographic or video evidence of their existence. For example, a photograph of a ghost goes missing for no reason, a processed camera film is completely blank or a video tape of ghost phenomena wipes itself clean for no reason.

KHU
An ancient Egyptian word for a ghost.

LEY LINE
A straight line of aligned landmarks (such as tors, rocky outcrops and hills) occurring naturally in the landscape along which flows an unknown force, possibly related to electromagnetism. Ley lines occur naturally, but nearly always include additional sites built by man, such as castles or churches. These normally have spiritual or ritualistic importance, and include megalithic monuments, burial mounds and historic buildings.

MANES
A general term used by the Romans to describe ghosts.

MATERIALIZATION
A Stage 4 manifestation that has enough energy to become physically real in the living world.

MEDIUM
Someone who is sensitive to ghosts and is unusually receptive to them. Some mediums relay messages supposedly from the other side, others use their power to aid psychic investigations. Most mediums have the ability to become temporarily possessed by a ghost and to allow the ghost to speak through them. The paranormal community is fraught with fake mediums who prey on vulnerable people, so use caution before engaging their services.

ORB
A commonly used term for a Stage 1 energy genesis.

OTHER SIDE
In many beliefs, the other side is the place where spirits go when the body dies. In broader terms, it is also used to describe a place where anything believed to remain after death exists. Also known as the afterworld.

OUIJA BOARD
A circular board with the letters of the alphabet on it that sometimes also contains key words, such as 'Yes' and 'No'. Ouija boards are used to contact the spirits of the dead, who supposedly spell out messages to the living by moving an upturned glass or planchette over the letters on the board. Ouija boards are often regarded as a children's game and, indeed, started out as a Victorian pastime. They should not, however, be taken lightly, as they can disturb the minds of sensitive individuals and some children. Ouija boards can also affect the *genius loci* of a place. The word 'ouija' comes from the French and German words for 'Yes': 'Oui' and 'Ja'.

PARANORMAL INDUCTION
The introduction of a spirit entity to a new location by the spirit attaching itself to a person or persons and travelling with them to a new site.

PASSING CONDITIONS
Physical symptoms inflicted temporarily on a medium or psychic by a ghost entity. The conditions vary from case to case, but are normally connected with conditions experienced by the dead entity at their time of death. Passing conditions sometimes linger for a short while after the communication has ceased before fading away.

PINPOINT LIGHTS
Dots of light often experienced at haunted locations. These are often recorded as being seen when a ghost is trying to manifest. The lights dart around in an apparently random manner and are normally azure blue or white in colour.

PSYCHIC EPICENTRE
The point where psychic energy is most highly focused. This can be a room, an area or a physical object.

RADIOTELETHESIS
This is where a witness takes on the feelings of the ghost. This can be an emotion, a physical pain connected with the death of the ghost or the ghost's fear of the witness. It is different from clairsentience in that it is involuntary and uncontrolled.

SÉANCE
A controlled attempt to communicate with the dead, usually involving a group of people who concentrate in a combined effort.

SPIRIT EXTRA
The term used to describe visible ghosts in photographs – used in the Victorian era when fake ghost photography was at its peak.

TABLE TILTING
The inexplicable tilting of tables, apparently of their own accord, but believed to be a form of communication from the dead. Table tilting normally takes place during a séance.

TASH/THEVSHI
Irish words for ghosts.

TELLURIC ENERGY
Energy of an unknown origin, but believed to come from the Earth. Also known as 'free energy' and 'earth energy'. Telluric is a derivative of 'tellurian', meaning 'terrestrial'.

TELLURIC ENERGY FIELD
A point at which telluric energy gathers, such as a ley-line convergence, a window area or a megalithic site (e.g. Stonehenge). A telluric energy field can span a large area from the energy centre (i.e. the standing stones, convergence point, etc.) and can be sensed by psychics at a considerable distance from the source.

TIMESLIP
A rip in the fabric of time whereby the past or future slips into the present and is experienced audibly, visually or, sometimes, physically by people from the present. Timeslips often occur on or near ley lines.

TRIGGER PERSON
A person whose very presence can induce paranormal activity.

VIGIL
Another term for a ghost hunt or investigation.

WINDOW AREA
A location where the ether is such that it may be exploited by supernatural forces to a greater extent than in other areas. Window areas can be created by uncontrolled use of a ouija board, occult ritual or black magic and, in some cases, the confluence of two or more ley lines.

Buildings or locations on single ley lines can also become window areas if they are subjected to occult practices or extreme attention is drawn to them for their 'paranormal' interest. For example, if lots of people come to a building to see and discuss ghosts, then the location itself becomes a magnet for ethereal presences and may become a window area.

BIBLIOGRAPHY

At the last count my library of books on the subject of ghosts and hauntings had reached 750 volumes. Here, I have selected the very best, which I have no hesitation in recommending to anyone with an interest in ghosts and hauntings. In particular, I recommend any works by Peter Underwood, Harry Price, Hans Holzer, Troy Taylor, John & Anne Spencer, Terence Whitaker, Jack Hallam, Elliott O'Donnell, Andrew Green, Sir Simon Marsden, Tony Cornell, Marc Alexander, Guy Lyon Playfair, Maurice Grosse and Jenny Randles.

Alexander, Marc *Haunted Houses You May Visit*

Banks, Ivan *The Enigma of Borley Rectory*
Bardens, Dennis *Ghosts & Hauntings*
Brooks, J. A. *Britain's Haunted Heritage*
Brooks, John *The Good Ghost Guide*
Burks, Eddie and Cribbs, Gillian *Ghost Hunter*

Chadbourn, Mark *Testimony*
Cornell, Tony *Poltergeists*
Cornell, Tony *Investigating the Paranormal*

Green, Andrew *Ghosts of Today*
Green, Andrew *Our Haunted Kingdom*
Grosse, Maurice *This House is Haunted*

Haining, Peter *A Dictionary of Ghosts*
Hallam, Jack *The Ghosts' Who's Who*
Hapgood, Sarah *500 British Ghosts & Hauntings*
Hapgood, Sarah *The World's Ghost & Poltergeist Stories*
Harley-Lewis, Roy *Ghosts, Hauntings & The Supernatural World*
Hippisley Coxe, Antony D. *Haunted Britain*
Holzer, Hans *Ghosts of New England*
Holzer, Hans *Haunted House Album*
Holzer, Hans *Ghosts*
Holzer, Hans *Love Beyond the Grave*
Holzer, Hans *Ghosts I've Met*

Jones, Richard *Haunted Britain and Ireland*
Jones, Richard *Haunted Inns of Britain and Ireland*
Jones, Richard *Haunted Castles of Britain and Ireland*

Linahan, Liz *The North of England Ghost Trail*
Lyon Playfair, Guy *The Haunted Pub Guide*

Maple, Eric *Supernatural England*
Marsden, Sir Simon *The Haunted Realm*
Marsden, Sir Simon *The Journal of a Ghosthunter*
Marsden, Sir Simon *Phantoms of the Isles*
Marsden, Sir Simon *Venice – City of Haunting Dreams*
Mason, John *Haunted Heritage*
Mead, Robin *Weekend Haunts*
Michael of Greece, Prince *Living with Ghosts*

Norman, Diana *The Stately Ghosts of England*

O'Donnell, Elliott *Dangerous Ghosts*
O'Donnell, Elliott *Haunted Britain*
O'Donnell, Elliott *Scottish Ghost Stories*

Price, Harry *The Biography of a Ghost Hunter*
Price, Harry *The End of Borley Rectory*
Price, Harry *The Most Haunted House In Britain*
Poole, Keith B. *Britain's Haunted Heritage*
Poole, Keith B. *Unfamiliar Spirits*

Randles, Jenny *Strange But True?*
Randles, Jenny *Strange But True? Casebook*
St Aubyn, Astrid *Ghostly Encounters*
Seymour, Deryck *The Ghosts of Berry Pomeroy Castle*
Spencer, John and Anne *The Encyclopedia of Ghosts & Spirits, Vols I & II*
Spencer, John and Anne *The Ghost Handbook*
Spencer, John and Anne *Ghost Hunter's Guide to Britain*
Spencer, John and Anne *Ghost Watching*
Spencer, John and Anne *The Poltergeist Phenomenon*
Sutherland, Jonathan *Ghosts of Great Britain*

Taylor, Troy *The Ghost Hunter's Guidebook*
Taylor, Troy *Field Guide to Spirit Photography*

Underwood, Peter *A Host of Hauntings*
Underwood, Peter *The A–Z of British Ghosts*
Underwood, Peter *Borley Postscript*
Underwood, Peter *Exorcism!*
Underwood, Peter *Ghostly Encounters*
Underwood, Peter *Ghosts & How To See Them*
Underwood, Peter *Ghosts & Phantoms of the West*
Underwood, Peter *The Ghost Hunters*
Underwood, Peter *The Ghost Hunter's Guide*
Underwood, Peter *The Ghost Hunter's Handbook*
Underwood, Peter *The Ghosts of Borley*
Underwood, Peter *Ghosts of Cornwall*
Underwood, Peter *Ghosts of Devon*
Underwood, Peter *Ghosts of Dorset*
Underwood, Peter *Ghosts of Kent*
Underwood, Peter *Ghosts of North Devon*
Underwood, Peter *Ghosts of Somerset*
Underwood, Peter *Ghosts of Wales*
Underwood, Peter *Ghosts of Wiltshire*
Underwood, Peter *Guide to Ghosts & Haunted Places*
Underwood, Peter *Haunted London*
Underwood, Peter *Nights In Haunted Houses*
Underwood, Peter *No Common Task*
Underwood, Peter *This Haunted Isle*
Underwood, Peter *West Country Hauntings*

Webster, Ken *The Vertical Plane*
Whitaker, Terence *England's Ghostly Heritage*
Whitaker, Terence *Haunted England*
Wilson, Ian *In Search of Ghosts*
Wyley, Graham *Strange West Country Hauntings*

INDEX

STANDARD FORMS NEEDED FOR AN INVESTIGATION

WITNESS REPORT AND INTERVIEW

Name

Telephone number(s)

Email address

Address

Street

Town/City

County/State

Postcode/Zip Code

Location, including the full address, of the experience(s):

Date(s) on which you had the experience(s):

Please describe, in your own words and as fully as possible, the experience you had (please use an extra sheet if necessary):

Signed

Date

WITNESS INTERVIEW FORM

NAME OF WITNESS:

CASE:

LOCATION OF EVENT:

Please attempt to answer all the following questions. If a question seems irrelevant to this particular case, please ignore it.

1. When did you first experience the ghost(s), i.e. date, time of day, etc.?

2. What were the weather conditions at the time?

3. Were you alone at the time of the experience? If not, who was with you? Please give names and addresses.

4. Did your companion(s), if any, experience the phenomenon in any way?

5. If you experienced the phenomenon on more than one occasion, did it behave in the same way each time?

6. If your experience was a sighting, please describe the manner in which it appeared and disappeared.

7. If your experience was a sighting, please describe the lighting conditions at the time.

8. If a sighting occurred, did it appear to be solid or translucent?

9. If your experience was a sighting, did it appear in colour, black and white or negative?

10. If your experience was aural (sounds), please describe it in detail, giving any comments on any strange or unusual elements of the noise.

11. Did you know, or do you now know, of anyone else who has had a supernatural experience at the same location?

12. Were you expecting to have a paranormal experience at the location concerned?

13. Did you have an interest in the paranormal prior to your experience?

14. Did you recognize the sighting or sound as being that of someone you either know or once knew? Have you been able to identify the sighting from a photograph or some other source since the experience?

15. If you recognized the sighting or sound as someone you know or once knew, had that person been in your thoughts recently?

16. Did the entity speak to you or make any attempt to speak or communicate with you and did it make a gesture to you of any kind? If so, what do you think this means?

17. If it did speak to you, exactly what did it say? Please be precise.

18. Did you speak to the sighting or answer the sound? If you did, what did you say? Please be precise.

19. How did the ghost react, if at all?

20. How did you feel during and after the experience(s): frightened; sad, glad, puzzled or some other emotion? If you felt frightened and had more than one experience of the same kind, did you feel more or less frightened on the subsequent occasions?

21. Did the ghost's movement seem natural or unnatural?

22. Did you notice anything else unusual at the time, such as sudden and intense silence, unusual sounds or scents? If so, exactly what did you notice?

23. Did you feel any variation in temperature before or after you saw the sighting or heard the sound or while it was present? If so, please describe it.

24. Were you asleep, or nearly asleep at the time of the experience?

25. If you were asleep, what woke you?

26. If you were awake when the experience started, what was your frame of mind: relaxed, tense, bored, or some other state?

27. If you were awake when the experience commenced, what were you doing directly before the experience?

28. How did you feel immediately after the experience?

29. Was there an animal present during the experience? If so, how did it react during and after the experience?

30. Does the building/location/place where the experience took place have a reputation for being haunted? If it does, did you know about this prior to your experience?

31. Have you ever had any other paranormal experiences of any kind? If so, please give details.

32. Do you have good eyesight? Do you wear glasses or contact lenses? If so, were you wearing them at the time of the experience? Are you long/short sighted? Are you colour-blind?

33. Are you epileptic? Is there any history of epilepsy in your immediate family?

34. Had you drunk alcohol, taken medicines or non-prescription drugs during the 24 hours prior to the experience? If so, please give details.

35. How do you feel about media publicity about your experience?

36. To whom did you first relate the experience? Please give their name and address.

37. Were you experiencing any kind of emotional difficulty prior to the experience? If so, please give details.

38. Has the experience caused you emotional distress since the incident? If so, in what way?

Signed:

Date:

STANDARD FORMS NEEDED FOR AN INVESTIGATION

WITNESS REPORT AND INTERVIEW

Name

Telephone number(s)

Email address

Address

Street

Town/City

County/State

Postcode/Zip Code

Location including full address at which you had the experience(s):

Date or dates on which you had the experience(s):

Please describe in your own words and as fully as possible, the experience you had (please use an extra sheet if necessary):

Signed

Date

WITNESS INTERVIEW FORM

NAME OF WITNESS:

CASE:

LOCATION OF EVENT:

Please attempt to answer all the following questions. If a question seems irrelevant to this particular case, please ignore it.

1. When did you first experience the ghost(s), i.e. date, time of day, etc.?

2. What were the weather conditions at the time?

3. Were you alone at the time of the experience? If not, who was with you? Please give names and addresses.

4. Did your companion(s), if any, experience the phenomenon in any way?

5. If you experienced the phenomenon on more than one occasion, did it behave in the same way each time?

6. If your experience was a sighting, please describe the manner in which it appeared and disappeared.

7. If your experience was a sighting, please describe the lighting conditions at the time.

8. If a sighting occurred, did it appear to be solid or translucent?

9. If your experience was a sighting, did it appear in colour, black and white or negative?

10. If your experience was aural (sounds), please describe it in detail, giving any comments on any strange or unusual elements of the noise.

11. Did you know, or do you now know, of anyone else who has had a supernatural experience at the same location?

12. Were you expecting to have a paranormal experience at the location concerned?

13. Did you have an interest in the paranormal prior to your experience?

14. Did you recognize the sighting or sound as being that of someone you either know or once knew? Have you been able to identify the sighting from a photograph or some other source since the experience?

15. If you recognized the sighting or sound as someone you know or once knew, had that person been in your thoughts recently?

16. Did the entity speak to you or make any attempt to speak or communicate with you and did it make a gesture to you of any kind? If so, what do you think this means?

17. If it did speak to you, exactly what did it say? Please be precise.

18. Did you speak to the sighting or answer the sound? If you did, what did you say? Please be precise.

19. How did the ghost react, if at all?

20. How did you feel during and after the experience(s): frightened; sad, glad, puzzled or some other emotion? If you felt frightened and had more than one experience of the same kind, did you feel more or less frightened on the subsequent occasions?

21. Did the ghost's movement seem natural or unnatural?

22. Did you notice anything else unusual at the time, such as sudden and intense silence, unusual sounds or scents? If so, exactly what did you notice?

23. Did you feel any variation in temperature before or after you saw the sighting or heard the sound or while it was present? If so, please describe it.

24. Were you asleep, or nearly asleep at the time of the experience?

25. If you were asleep, what woke you?

26. If you were awake when the experience started, what was your frame of mind: relaxed, tense, bored, or some other state?

27. If you were awake when the experience commenced, what were you doing directly before the experience?

28. How did you feel immediately after the experience?

29. Was there an animal present during the experience? If so, how did it react during and after the experience?

30. Does the building/location/place where the experience took place have a reputation for being haunted? If it does, did you know about this prior to your experience?

31. Have you ever had any other paranormal experiences of any kind? If so, please give details.

32. Do you have good eyesight? Do you wear glasses or contact lenses? If so, were you wearing them at the time of the experience? Are you long/short sighted? Are you colour-blind?

33. Are you epileptic? Is there any history of epilepsy in your immediate family?

34. Had you drunk alcohol, taken medicines or non-prescription drugs during the 24 hours prior to the experience? If so, please give details.

35. How do you feel about media publicity about your experience?

36. To whom did you first relate the experience? Please give their name and address.

37. Were you experiencing any kind of emotional difficulty prior to the experience? If so, please give details.

38. Has the experience caused you emotional distress since the incident? If so, in what way?

Signed:

Date:

STANDARD FORMS NEEDED FOR AN INVESTIGATION

WITNESS REPORT AND INTERVIEW

Name

Telephone number(s)

Email address

Address

Street

Town/City

County/State

Postcode/Zip Code

Location including full address at which you had the experience(s):

Date or dates on which you had the experience(s):

Please describe in your own words and as fully as possible, the experience you had (please use an extra sheet if necessary):

Signed

Date

WITNESS INTERVIEW FORM

NAME OF WITNESS:

CASE:

LOCATION OF EVENT:

Please attempt to answer all the following questions. If a question seems irrelevant to this particular case, please ignore it.

1. When did you first experience the ghost(s), i.e. date, time of day, etc.?

2. What were the weather conditions at the time?

3. Were you alone at the time of the experience? If not, who was with you? Please give names and addresses.

4. Did your companion(s), if any, experience the phenomenon in any way?

5. If you experienced the phenomenon on more than one occasion, did it behave in the same way each time?

6. If your experience was a sighting, please describe the manner in which it appeared and disappeared.

7. Where you expecting to have a paranormal experience at the location concerned?

8. If your experience was a sighting, please describe the lighting conditions at the time.

9. If your experience was aural (sounds), please describe it in detail, giving any comments on any strange or unusual elements of the noise.

10. If a sighting occurred, did it appear to be solid or translucent?

11. Did you know, or do you now know, of anyone else who has had a supernatural experience at the same location?

12. If a sighting occurred, did it appear in colour, black and white or negative?

13. Did you have an interest in the paranormal prior to your experience?

14. Did you recognize the sighting or voice as being that of someone you either know or once knew? Have you been able to identify the sighting from a photograph or some other source since the experience?

15. If you recognized the sighting or voice as someone you know or did know, had that person been in your thoughts recently?

16. Did the entity speak to you or make any attempt to speak or communicate with you and did it make a gesture to you of any kind? If so, what do you think this means?

17. If it did speak to you, exactly what did it say? Please be precise.

18. Did you speak to the sighting or answer the voice? If you did, what did you say? Please be precise.

19. How did the ghost react, if at all?

20. How did you feel during and after the experience(s): frightened; sad, glad, puzzled or some other emotion? If you felt frightened and had more than one experience of the same kind, did you feel more or less frightened on the subsequent occasions?

21. Did the ghost's movement seem natural or unnatural?

22. Did you notice anything else unusual at the time, such as sudden and intense silence, unusual sounds or scents? If so, exactly what did you notice?

23. Did you feel any variation in temperature before or after you saw sighting or heard the voice or while it was present? If so, please describe it.

24. Were you asleep, or nearly asleep at the time of the experience?

25. If you were asleep, what woke you?

26. If you were awake when the experience started, what was your frame of mind: relaxed, tense, bored, or some other state?

27. If you were awake when the experience commenced, what were you doing directly before the experience?

28. How did you feel immediately after the experience?

29. Was there an animal present during the experience? If so, how did it react during and after the experience?

30. Does the building/location/place where the experience took place have a reputation for being haunted? If it does, did you know about this prior to your experience?

31. Have you ever had any other paranormal experiences of any kind? If so, please give details.

32. Do you have good eyesight? Do you wear glasses or contact lenses? If so, were you wearing them at the time of the experience? Are you long/short sighted? Are you colour-blind?

33. Are you epileptic? Is there any history of epilepsy in your immediate family?

34. Had you drunk alcohol, taken medicines or non-prescription drugs during the 24 hours prior to the experience? If so, please give details.

35. How do you feel about media publicity about your experience?

36. To whom did you first relate the experience? Please give their name and address.

37. Were you experiencing any kind of emotional difficulty prior to the experience? If so, please give details.

38. Has the experience caused you emotional distress since the incident? If so, in what way?

Signed:

Date:

STANDARD FORMS NEEDED FOR AN INVESTIGATION

WITNESS REPORT AND INTERVIEW

Name

Telephone number(s)

Email address

Address

Street

Town/City

County/State

Postcode/Zip Code

Location including full address at which you had the experience(s):

Date or dates on which you had the experience(s):

Please describe in your own words and as fully as possible, the experience you had (please use an extra sheet if necessary):

Signed

Date

WITNESS INTERVIEW FORM

NAME OF WITNESS:

CASE:

LOCATION OF EVENT:

Please attempt to answer all the following questions. If a question seems irrelevant to this particular case, please ignore it.

1. When did you first experience the ghost(s), i.e. date, time of day, etc.?

2. What were the weather conditions at the time?

3. Were you alone at the time of the experience? If not, who was with you? Please give names and addresses.

4. Did your companion(s), if any, experience the phenomenon in any way?

5. If you experienced the phenomenon on more than one occasion, did it behave in the same way each time?

6. If your experience was a sighting, please describe the manner in which it appeared and disappeared.

7. If your experience was a sighting, please describe the lighting conditions at the time.

8. If a sighting occurred, did it appear to be solid or translucent?

9. If your experience was a sighting, did it appear in colour, black and white or negative?

10. If your experience was aural (sounds), please describe it in detail, giving any comments on any strange or unusual elements of the noise.

11. Did you know, or do you now know, of anyone else who has had a supernatural experience at the same location?

12. Were you expecting to have a paranormal experience at the location concerned?

13. Did you have an interest in the paranormal prior to your experience?

14. Did you recognize the sighting or sound as being that of someone you either know or once knew? Have you been able to identify the sighting from a photograph or some other source since the experience?

15. If you recognized the sighting or sound as someone you know or once knew, had that person been in your thoughts recently?

16. Did the entity speak to you or make any attempt to speak or communicate with you and did it make a gesture to you of any kind? If so, what do you think this means?

17. If it did speak to you, exactly what did it say? Please be precise.

18. Did you speak to the sighting or answer the sound? If you did, what did you say? Please be precise.

19. How did the ghost react, if at all?

20. How did you feel during and after the experience(s): frightened; sad, glad, puzzled or some other emotion? If you felt frightened and had more than one experience of the same kind, did you feel more or less frightened on the subsequent occasions?

21. Did the ghost's movement seem natural or unnatural?

22. Did you notice anything else unusual at the time, such as sudden and intense silence, unusual sounds or scents? If so, exactly what did you notice?

23. Did you feel any variation in temperature before or after you saw the sighting or heard the sound or while it was present? If so, please describe it.

24. Were you asleep, or nearly asleep at the time of the experience?

25. If you were asleep, what woke you?

26. If you were awake when the experience started, what was your frame of mind: relaxed, tense, bored, or some other state?

27. If you were awake when the experience commenced, what were you doing directly before the experience?

28. How did you feel immediately after the experience?

29. Was there an animal present during the experience? If so, how did it react during and after the experience?

30. Does the building/location/place where the experience took place have a reputation for being haunted? If it does, did you know about this prior to your experience?

31. Have you ever had any other paranormal experiences of any kind? If so, please give details.

32. Do you have good eyesight? Do you wear glasses or contact lenses? If so, were you wearing them at the time of the experience? Are you long/short sighted? Are you colour-blind?

33. Are you epileptic? Is there any history of epilepsy in your immediate family?

34. Had you drunk alcohol, taken medicines or non-prescription drugs during the 24 hours prior to the experience? If so, please give details.

35. How do you feel about media publicity about your experience?

36. To whom did you first relate the experience? Please give their name and address.

37. Were you experiencing any kind of emotional difficulty prior to the experience? If so, please give details.

38. Has the experience caused you emotional distress since the incident? If so, in what way?

Signed:

Date:

PICTURE ACKNOWLEDGEMENTS

All photographs supplied by Jason Karl except:
Courtesy of Amberley Castle Hotel: Pages 128–9
Jennifer Chance: Page 14
Chris Coe: Pages 115, 134
Courtesy of Culcreuch Castle: Page 135
The Fortean Picture Library: Pages 24, 28, 30, 49, 84
Ian French: Pages 10, 26, 64, 104
The Illustrated London News: Page 22
Richard Jones: Page 53
Courtesy of Llancaiach Fawr: Page 107
Mary Evans Picture Library: Pages 39, 44, 47, 50, 51, 80
Simon Marsden: Pages 69–71, 122
Alan Marshall: Pages 3, 27, 34, 36, 113, 117, 119, 121
John Mason: Pages 29, 45, 101, 109, 95
Courtesy of The Mermaid Inn, Rye: Page 133
Norie Miles: Page 15
Courtesy of Muncaster Castle: Pages 105, 106
Catherine Plant: Page 16
Pure Television Ltd: Pages 65, 76
David Tipling: Page 19
Elizabeth Udall: Pages 66–8, 137

AUTHOR ACKNOWLEDGEMENTS

I am indebted to those who have accompanied me around Britain on my ghostly adventures, often spending hours in cold and uncomfortable buildings waiting for the unimaginable to appear.

I would also like to thank the following people for their help in producing this book:

Everyone at The Ghost Research Foundation International past and present, especially Veronica Charles, Paul Howse, Norie Miles, Lyndi and Matt Telepneff, Justine Yarwood, Paul Browne, Elaine O'Regan, Judy Farncombe, Diana Jarvis, Angela Borrows, Diane Lawrence, Sybil Lucas-Brewer, Richard Taylor, Daniel Holmes, Wendy O'Connor, Carla Schmitz, Helen Johnson and Drew Crow Star (Drew especially for sharing a terrifying evening at a haunted flat in London – not so much caused by ghosts, more so by the living!).

I would also like to thank my Grandmother Dee for answering the phones from day one, Julia Hodson, Philippa Young and Patrick Cooke of Athelhampton Hall, *Psychic News* and in particular Lyn Guest de Swarte, The Ghost Club Society, The National Trust, English Heritage, Eleanor O'Keefe and The Society for Psychical Research, Jonathan Hancock of BBC Radio Oxford, Julie Rose and all 'my ladies' at Banbury Museum, Jane Lee, Linda Wright and Robert Holtom of Ettington Park Hotel, Peter Underwood for being my inspiration and for writing a perfect Foreword, Graham Wyley for supplying a copy of his wonderful book, Marion Goodfellow for her friendship and for writing a great Afterword, Suzanne Le Fayre and Joyce Thorne for their never-ending help, Ian French for his excellent ghost photographs, John Mason for his outstanding haunting images, Victor and Solange Tobutt and Tamsyn of The Wellington Hotel, Sally and Bruce Thompson of the Highwayman Inn for their friendship and support, and Judith Blincow of The Mermaid Inn for supplying a fantastic picture.

And lastly I would like to thank my Mum and Dad, Elizabeth and Barrie, for putting up with a 'spooky' child for 18 years!